1

ALFA ROMEO SPORTS COUPÉS
1954–1989

The Classic Pedigree

Other Titles in the Crowood AutoClassics Series

Alfa Romeo Sports Coupés 1954–1989

The Classic Pedigree

Graham Robson

The Crowood Press

First published in 2002 by
The Crowood Press Ltd
Ramsbury, Marlborough
Wiltshire SN8 2HR

British Library Cataloguing-in-Publication Data
A catalogue record for this book is available from the British Library.

ISBN 1 86126 507 7

Typeset by Naomi Lunn

Printed and bound in Great Britain by Bookcraft, Midsomer Norton

Contents

Coupé Evolution 1954–89

April 1954	Launch of Bertone-styled Giulietta Sprint, at Turin Motor Show.
Late 1954	First deliveries of Giulietta Sprint.
April 1956	Launch of Giulietta Sprint Veloce.
November 1957	Introduction of prototype Giulietta Sprint Speciale, with styling by Bertone.
1959	General Giulietta upgrade from '750' Chassis sequence to '101' Chassis type.
March 1960	Official launch of the Zagato-styled Giulietta SZ.
Mid-1962	Last deliveries of Giulietta Sprint/Sprint Veloce types. Introduction of Giulia 1600 Sprint.
September 1963	Introduction of the Giulia Sprint GT, with 106bhp/1,570cc.
March 1964	Reintroduction of 1.3-litre-engined Giulietta coupé, the 1300 Sprint.
Early 1965	Last deliveries of the original Bertone-styled car, the 1300 Sprint.
March 1966	Launch of the 109bhp Giulia Sprint GT Veloce, to replace the 106bhp Giulia Sprint GT.
January 1968	Introduction of the 1750 GT Veloce, as a direct replacement for the Giulia Sprint GT Veloce.
June 1971	Introduction of the 2000 GT Veloce, soon to take over from the 1750 GT Veloce, withdrawn at the end of the year.
Mid-1972	Reintroduction of a 1.6-litre-engined Giulia Sprint GT, the GT 1600 Junior.
May 1974	Introduction of the original Alfetta GT (a 1.8-litre model).
May 1976	Alfetta GT 1.8 discontinued. Replaced by Alfetta 1.6 and Alfetta GTV 2000 models.
Mid-1976	All Giulia-style Sprint GT derivatives finally discontinued.
September 1976	Introduction of original Alfasud Sprint, with 1.3-litre engine.
August 1978	Introduction of Sud Sprint 1350 and 1500 types.
Mid-1980	Introduction of Sud Sprint GT Veloce types.
November 1980	Introduction of Alfetta GTV6 (with V6 engine), along with interior restyle for GTV 2000. Alfetta GT 1.6 discontinued.
Spring 1983	Introduction of Sud Sprint Green Cloverleaf derivative.
1986	End of series production of Alfetta GT and GTV6 models (200 special 3-litre-engined GTV6s would be built in 1987, for the South African market).
End 1987/ early 1988	Launch of Sud Sprint with 1.7-litre engine.
January 1989	Sud Sprint discontinued.

Introduction

I have often thought that Alfa Romeo's many classic coupés – the closed cars which have sold so widely, and for so many years – have been overshadowed by the even more racy open-top sports cars. Yet many more Alfa coupés than open-top sports cars have always been sold.

The famous Alfa Romeo coupé pedigree, once established in the 1930s, has been handed down from generation to generation, which explains why the Giulietta Sprint can be compared so easily with the Alfetta GT, or the Giulia Sprint GT with the Sud Sprint. Why? Just for a moment, consider a few model names – Sprint Veloce, Bertone Sprint Speciale, Tubulare Zagato, GTV6 and Green Cloverleaf among them – and add in the designers' credits, Bertone and Giugiaro. What other car-maker can boast of exciting links like those?

Isn't it amazing, therefore, that the careers of these Alfa Romeo coupés have never previously been covered in one volume? This omission, and my· long-lasting love of Alfa Romeo products, inspired me to write this book. However, although this is a story that really began in the 1930s, it only became commercially significant in the mid-1950s, when the much-loved Giulietta Sprint went on sale. As a result, my strategy has been to describe, and to compare in detail, the Alfa Romeo coupés built in the second half of the twentieth century.

It has, of course, been a real pleasure, for Alfa Romeo has the type of glamorous brand image that its rivals would kill for. And it has remained consistent: an image established in the 1920s when the Grand Prix cars swept all before them, has been maintained to this day. For much of that time, the company has produced fast and sporting road cars to feed their clients' desires. Large cars, small cars, open cars and closed cars – all have carried the famous badge, and all have provided the sort of motoring excitement that has seen the world's enthusiasts queuing up to buy them, to enjoy their characters, and to love them in spite of their shortcomings. These are the cars which I describe so affectionately in the following pages.

Graham Robson

1 Alfa's Coupé Heritage

What do you look for in a car? Tradition? Image? Style? A sporting record? Think of Alfa Romeo and you won't go far wrong.

Alfa Romeo, in my opinion, is a car-making company unlike any other. No car lover has ever been indifferent to the marque. In a long and eventful life, Alfa Romeo has packed in so much – great cars, ordinary cars, cars that succeeded and cars that failed. There have been profits and near bankruptcies; devastation and new beginnings; independence and corporate rescues.

Life and progress has rarely been humdrum and, somehow, Alfa Romeo has managed to pack in every type of activity: sports cars, racing cars, coupés, and not forgetting the saloons that made the money, the light commercial vehicles that surprised everyone, and the aircraft engines which impressed everyone who sampled them.

The company has a long history, but I am not about to impose it on you in its entirety. Although Alfa Romeo's heritage influenced the coupés that evolved from the 1950s, they stand on their own as technical and marketing marvels.

Influences

The first cars of this pedigree were Alfas – not Alfa Romeos – made in Milan from 1910; mining engineer Nicola Romeo did not get involved until 1914, so the famous Alfa Romeo marque did not truly emerge until the end of the First World War. Even by that time, the first sporting Alfas were on sale, and the first twin-cam racing engine had made its debut in a Grand Prix car in 1914. A legend was already being established.

It was not until the 1950s that Alfa Romeo built large numbers of cars. In the 1920s, peak

---

Twin-Cam Engine Tradition

Alfa Romeo was a pioneer of the use of twin-overhead camshaft engines, both in motorsport and in road cars. The very first twin-cam-engined Alfa Romeo was the 1914 Grand Prix car, and the first limited-production road car was the 6C 1500 Sport of 1928. After that, the tradition of twin-cam Alfas was well established, though annual production was always very small – 699 cars were made in 1934, a mere 42 in 1939.

Volume production of twin-cams began in 1950, when the four-cylinder/90bhp 1900 saloon was launched. More than 17,000 were built in three years, an achievement which changed the face of Alfa Romeo. At that time, the only other automotive twin-cam engine in series production came from Jaguar in the UK.

The new-generation, later famous, four-cylinder twin-cam engine which powered almost every model described in this book, first appeared in 1954 in the Giulietta Sprint. It was fitted to sports cars, Spiders, saloons and light commercial vehicles in the next two decades, and soon became the world's best-selling twin-cam. The final derivatives of this famous engine were not built until the early 1990s, when the last of the legendary Giulia-based 2000 Spiders was assembled.

---

production of 1,110 was achieved in 1925, and in the 1930s the best achieved was a mere 699 in 1934. Along the way, the company's finances collapsed in 1933, rescue from the Government-financed Istituto Ricostruzione Industriale (Institute of Industrial Reconstruction/IRI) followed, and activity turned towards military rather than private-car needs. Because Alfa Romeo came to rely on aircraft engine orders for its business, in some years the private cars almost disappeared from view – only ten new cars were produced in 1936, and only forty-two in 1939.

Yet, in all that time, Alfa Romeo never built a boring car. Some were too complicated and some were too heavy, but none of them was ignored. Nuvolari and 1750 Gran Sports, Tipo B single-seaters prepared by Enzo Ferrari, incredible twin-engined racing cars, and future stars like Dr Guiseppe Farina in Alfettas made headlines in motorsport. On the road, rich men throughout Europe bought individually erected, glossy, eight-cylinder, supercharged monsters such as the 8C 2300 and 8C 2900B models, all of which were distinguished by their exotic coachwork.

Coupés

Coupés as we know them did not really emerge until the 1920s, and it was only in post-war years that they became at all common. Almost all early cars carried open-top coachwork – from two-seats up to a gargantuan eight seats or more – but by the end of the 1900s, saloons and limousines had come to dominate. Sports cars, as such, evolved in the 1910s, and came into their own in the 1920s.

Once Europe's motor industry settled down in the 1920s, most cars seemed to be saloons, limousines, tourers or two-seater sports cars. This did not persist for long, and it was soon time for the arrival of the 'coupé'. The name is derived from the French word *coupé*, which refers to something that has been cut or chopped. Accordingly, it was French coachbuilders who took that word into their vocabulary, using it to refer to a car in which the normal roof had been cut down or chopped. By custom, if not by accurate definition, the 'coupé' was eventually applied to two-door cars

Before there were Alfa coupés there were out-and-out Alfa sports cars. In the early 1930s, none was more fierce than the supercharged 8C 2300 type, this being Tazio Nuvolari on his way to winning the Mille Miglia in 1933.

with a permanently fixed roof and more rakish lines than the saloon. Such cars were often light-ly modified, or further evolved, versions of tour-ers or even sports cars.

At this point various sub-divisions of car began to evolve, and the definitions became blurred. Drop-head coupés were cars with folding tops and – usually – two doors, these being more civ-ilized derivatives of tourers, while the Americans then began to talk about 'hardtop coupés', which sometimes had four passenger doors.

Even so, just about every nation seemed to agree that a true coupé was more rakish than a saloon, would always have more flowing lines, might sometimes have two seats but more often had four. The mass-market took years to develop (Detroit was first), which left independent coach-builders with a chance to corner the European market.

Coupés were rare at first – and expensive. Though most of Alfa Romeo's famous 1750s were open tourers or outright sports cars, one or two fixed-head coupés were developed. As the 1920s turned into the 1930s, the numbers began to increase – but only slowly. Quite simply, a closed coupé might have been a more civilized, high-speed form of transport than a tourer or a drop-head, but it was not yet fashionable.

Several Italian coachbuilders – Bertone and Stabilimenti Farina of Turin; Zagato and Touring of Milan, among them – spotted the same trends, and each moved in their own way to satisfy the demand, and before the end of the 1930s had made exclusive (small) numbers of true Alfa Romeo coupés. From the mid-1930s, a series of stunning, rounded shapes on 6C 2300B, 6C 2500 and 8C 2900B types – some for motor racing, some for road use – entranced all who saw them.

Post-War Developments

When Germany invaded Poland on 1 September 1939, the world changed forever. For years, no-one could forecast what would happen after-wards. What had been socially acceptable in the 1930s might not even survive into a post-war period.

It took six years, millions of deaths, and much devastation to end the madness. On 8 May 1945, citizens of Europe woke up to the realization that the shelling, the bombing and the killing had stopped – and that their old way of life had been destroyed. In the aftermath of the fighting, it became clear that there was not the scope for sell-ing the same sort of luxury goods as in the 1930s. With civilization, however fragile, to be restored,

---

State Control

In its earlier days, Alfa Romeo never made much money. By the early 1930s, as Europe struggled to shrug off a deep depression inspired by the Wall Street Crash of 1929, the money began to run out. It was not just that Alfa Romeo did not sell many road cars, but that it spent so much on a high-profile (and successful) racing programme.

By 1933, bankruptcy was looming, yet because the company was also heavily involved in making aero-engines and trucks for Italy's burgeoning military forces, this could not be allowed to happen. Italy's then Fascist dictator, Benito Mussolini, wanted Alfa Romeo to survive, not only as one of his arsenals, but as a way of preserving Italy's prestige in international motorsport. And he already had a way of ensuring this.

An organization titled the Istituto Ricostruzione Industriale had been set up by Mussolini's government, backed with almost unlimited public funds, to mould the country to the Dictator's political will. Accordingly, in 1933 it was the IRI who took control of Alfa Romeo – it was not outright nationalization, because the company still kept its own board of directors – underpinned the company's finances and made sure that the prestige/military aspect of the com-pany was henceforth dominant.

For the next ten years, the IRI's role was benevolent, but it also provided the reason for the destruction of the Portel-lo (Milan) factory during the Second World War. Because Alfa Romeo had become a massive military machinery com-plex, the Allied bombers made haste to lay it to ruins – which they achieved in 1943 and 1944.

Even so, the IRI, in post-war democratized form, remained in control of Alfa Romeo until the 1980s, when a sale was finally made to Fiat (*see* page 179).

Coupé trends became established at Alfa Romeo before the end of the 1930s, this being the very exclusive – and expensive – Touring-bodied 8C 2900B of 1937–39.

and with much damage to be repaired, it made more sense to concentrate on mundane matters. Utilitarian products at low prices, rather than glossy indulgences, were needed.

Although Alfa Romeo's bosses, who included the distinguished Dr Ing. Orazio Satta Puliga as its Technical Chief, realized this, they were powerless to do anything appropriate. For one thing, the company had never produced run-of-the-mill machinery and, for another, neither time nor the availability of capital was on their side. With at least 60 per cent of the factory at Portello now destroyed – it had been systematically flattened by Allied bombing – the challenge was, quite simply, to produce *anything*. The priority was to repair the Portello buildings; after that the surviving workforce would have to tackle anything

that brought in cash – and only then could new cars be produced.

Amazingly, some of the tooling and most of the expertise capable of building the pre-war Alfa Romeo cars was reassembled in Milan. With no prospect of making new models, as far as Alfa Romeo was concerned, those cars could only be lightly improved versions of the 1939 models. The six-cylinder-engined 6C 2500 had been launched in 1939 (it was a direct descendant of the earlier 6C 2300B of 1937–39), and by 1945 a total of 761 such machines had been manufactured, almost all of them during the war years when the company was otherwise concentrating on producing aircraft engines. Of that total, 152 had been Coloniales (military staff cars), and many were five- or six-seater saloons, but a good

---

After the Bombing

Although Alfa Romeo was involved in making military aero-engines in the late 1930s, few of its staff ever wanted to see Italy go to war. For a time, after Mussolini declared war on France and Britain in 1940, the factories were safe, but once the Allies' long-range bombers were ready in 1942–43, the skies over Milan became dangerous.

First in February 1943, again in August 1943, and repeatedly in 1944, the Portello factory was systematically bombarded, so that little was left standing when peace was declared in May 1945. As with BMW, Mercedes-Benz and VW in Germany, the factory was ruined, most of the tooling and machinery destroyed, and many key staff were lost in the fighting.

The renaissance which followed was slow but desperate. First of all the rubble was cleared, the surviving facilities cleaned up, and a skeleton staff reassembled. For a time there was little to be done except tackle the repairs of badly run-down cars and trucks in Milan. Then, in 1946, the first private post-war cars – 6C 2500s of pre-war design – were delivered, and things gradually began to return to normal.

But times had changed in Europe: the market for big, glossy and expensive cars had contracted. Alfa's controllers, the IRI, therefore encouraged a change of strategy – to build a new series of smaller-engined, simpler-engineered, and therefore cheaper new cars. But it would be years before any of them could be made available.

The records show just how difficult the post-war recovery actually was. Only 162 6C 2500 types were built in 1946, and a peak of 467 followed in 1949. The all-new, cheaper saloon type – the 1900 – then appeared, but only 1,228 were produced in 1951, and 5,411 in 1953 (the best achieved by that model).

The fact that the Tipo 158 and Tipo 159 Grand Prix Alfa Romeos were still the world's best was heart-warming, but did nothing for the financial situation, and the only way to break out, it seemed, was for another, even smaller, even cheaper range of Alfas to be developed. Thus the Giulietta was born.

Even then, Portello's limitations were already obvious. Surrounded as it was by houses and other buildings in industrial Milan, it could never be expanded, which explains why, when the Giulia range came along in 1962, a brand new factory at Arese, a few miles outside Milan, was erected.

---

number had been elegant two-door machines, many with gloriously sleek fixed-head coupé bodies by Touring. With 90bhp from their 2.5-litre twin-cam engines, these could achieve 100mph (161kph), and were prestigious indeed.

So, if Alfa Romeo was to get back into any type of private-car assembly, it would have to be 6C 2500s or nothing. So what if the mid-1940s economic climate was not right for such machines? Better to try and go down fighting than to turn to making hand carts, bicycles or domestic machinery.

Somehow, among the chaos, the rubble and the economic disarray, Alfa Romeo managed to produce three Touring-bodied 6C 2500 Sport coupés in 1945, followed by another sixty-eight Sports and fourteen 110bhp Super Sports in 1946. It was a typical piece of Italian *braggadocio* – all flashing eyes and puffed-out chest – as if Alfa Romeo was stating: OK, we know you can't sell cars like this any more, but we are going to do just that!

Thus it was that Alfa's coupé traditions, new in the 1920s and excitingly developed in the 1930s, came to fruition. Coupés with splendid styles, it seemed, would always be a part of Alfa's activities.

And in the next few years they became a very important part. To follow up the rebirth of the 6C 2500, in 1947 Alfa Romeo introduced a revised range, the coupé version of which they called the 6C 2500 '*Frecchia d'Oro*' ('Golden Arrow'). Not only did the saloon version of this car go partway towards modern construction, by having its body shells welded to the chassis frame, but there was a steering column gearchange – and revised styles.

For construction of a series of coupé types, rolling chassis of *Frecchia d'Oro* types were supplied to Touring (cabriolets were built by Pininfarina). Interestingly enough, at this stage neither Bertone nor Zagato were yet officially involved, though Bertone certainly built isolated examples.

Touring's approved style, which lasted from 1947 to 1952, set out many styling 'cues' which would be developed into the 1950s. Although

Carrozzeria Touring was one of Alfa's favoured coachbuilders in the late 1940s, and developed this magnificent two-door four-seater for the 6C 2500 'Freccia d'Oro' ('Golden Arrow') of 1947.

The 6C 2500 looked right from every angle. Although the Giulietta would come from a different styling house, some of the cues from this larger Touring shape would persist into the 1950s.

this shape went only partway towards a flush-panelled side (vestigial front 'wings' featured, fairing into the doors, halfway along the side of the car), the headlamps were fully recessed, as were the auxiliary driving lamps, there was a slim version of the Alfa Romeo 'shield' grille, and the rear quarters were smooth and curvaceous.

From 1947 to 1953, a grand total of 680 *Frecchia d'Oro* coupé types, and another 288 related sporty versions were produced from a factory that was increasingly modernized, and ever more confident in itself and its future.

These, though, had all been interim cars, with expensive-to-build twin-cam 2.5-litre engines of

Carrozzeria Touring's 'Villa d'Este' style on the 6C 2500 of 1952 was one of its most pleasing – but was really only a two-seater.

Another 6C 2500, and another style by Touring, dating from 1949.

a pre-war type. Although they were valuable in bridging the gap between Alfa Romeo's past and its future, they would have to be replaced some day.

1900 – the New Generation

That day came, at last, in 1950, when the company unveiled its very first true post-war model, the 1900. It was a car which would take the place of, but which could not replace, the 6C 2500, for it was completely different in its market aspirations.

Here, for the very first time, was a 'standard' Alfa Romeo, with four passenger doors and conventional saloon car styling – a long way from the 1930s, when almost every Alfa Romeo sold to the public was significantly different from any other.

It may have been a high risk strategy, but it worked. One statistic tells its own story. From 1939 to 1953, a total of 2,594 6C 2500s were produced. Yet from 1950 to 1959, no fewer than

21,304 1900 types were produced. One model change and a decisive move downmarket produced an eight-fold increase in sales.

The 6C 2500s had been expensive; 1900s were cheaper. The 6C 2500s had always been hand-built; 1900s were produced on increasingly sophisticated machinery. The 6C 2500s were always sold to the rich; 1900s went to the middle-classes. This was the sea-change in Alfa Romeo's strategy, long-forecast by the pundits, agreed in private by Alfa management in 1946, but which took four years to reach the public. Left on its own in 1945, Alfa would certainly have perished, but with massive aid (both from the IRI, and by huge reconstruction loans to Italy from the United States Marshall Aid programme), it survived.

One condition of the loans was that the company's cars would have to reach out to more middle-class, middle-income customers where potential sales were greater. Whatever was designed to replace the 6C 2500 would have to

Touring carried its expertise, and the same basic proportions as the 6C 2500, over to the unit-construction 1900, this being the 1900 Sprint of 1951. Very gradually, Alfa shapes were moving towards the more accessible styles of the 1950s.

be cheaper to build, would have to be built in larger numbers, and would have to feature modern engineering. Ing. Satta Puliga's team accepted this, but because of their lengthy traditions, they were not about to produce anything cheap and cheerful. The result was that, although the 1900 was a conventional-looking four-door saloon (certainly the styling flair of the 1930s Alfas was missing), it was still powered by a twin-cam engine, and it was equipped with a unit-construction (monocoque) body-chassis structure.

Previewed outside the Turin Motor Show of May 1950 (but not on a stand in the display itself), the 1900 might have looked mundane (its four-door lines were anonymous, slightly rounded, and not at all striking), but as a statement of technical intent it still caused a sensation. Its launch perhaps seems to have been premature (and made under pressure from its backers), for the company only briefly showed it off outside the hall, demonstrating it only to a favoured few, then withdrew it, stating that it would go on sale before the end of the year.

But here was a new model of a type which would be replicated many times in the next thirty years. Most important of all was that this was the first new model from Alfa Romeo with a unit-construction steel body shell – which, if only we had known it then, was going to make things difficult for special bodywork manufacturers in the future. Although much of the stiffness and rigidity of the new structure was concentrated in the box-section sills and the sturdy transmission tunnel, the entire cabin was welded together, and there was considerable strength in the way that windscreen pillars and roof cant-rail sections were laid out. Any specialist company wanting to produce unique styles would have to think deeply, and be prepared to invest heavily in new production methods.

By Alfa Romeo standards, though, the rest of the running gear was familiar, even conventional, enough. The 100bhp/1,884cc twin-cam engine (with its classic part-spherical combustion chambers, and chain-driven overhead camshafts which operated widely separated lines of inlet and exhaust valves) was at the front of the car, yet unhappily the then-fashionable steering column gearchange (thought to be attractive to North American customers) was provided.

The drive itself was through a four-speed gearbox to the rear wheels, and by comparison with the overcomplicated 6C 2500, the rear suspension design was simplicity itself – by a beam axle, located by coil springs, radius arms, and by an A-bracket tied to the top of the axle casing itself (prototype cars used trailing arms and a Panhard rod, but this was not satisfactory).

Although more compact than the old 6C 2500 models, the 1900 had a 103.5in (2,630mm) wheelbase, 52in (1,320mm) wheel tracks, and weighed in at 2,425lb (1,100kg). It was going to be a different type of Alfa – more solid and more sober than before (that, at least, is what its engineers hoped), but still with a 105mph (170kph) top speed.

Alfa Romeo-watchers were receptive enough, but immediately started asking awkward questions, such as 'When are we going to see the first sporting versions?' and 'When will we see the first special styles?' In the end they had to wait for both, for there would be no coupés before 1951, and no 115bhp 'Super' derivatives until 1953.

1900 Coupés

Traditionally, Alfa Romeo coupés and cabriolets had always been manufactured outside the factory – by specialists such as Touring, Pininfarina and Zagato – and always on the basis of cars which had their own self-supporting chassis frames. This was ingrained into their operating methods. The only real difference between the separate-chassis cars of the 1900s and those of the 1940s was in their general shape and their rigidity; no major advances in technology had ever been made.

Because the chassis were rigid enough, body shells could be relatively flimsy, and assembled round wooden or part-wood-part-steel body skeletons. When finished, they would be bolted – not welded – to the rolling chassis. Production runs tended to be limited; only the outer panels needed to be pressed or carefully formed, and it was always possible to change style without

Bertone finally got in on the Alfa act in the early 1950s, this being a neat two-door 2+2-seater coupé on the 1900 saloon platform of 1953.

Not all 1900 shapes were totally successful, this being accredited by Alfa's historical archive to 'Colli' in 1953. Only a year later Bertone's efforts on the Giulietta base would make it look very ordinary indeed.

spending huge amounts of capital on new press tools.

But that was then, and this was the 1950s. In Italy, where such body-building concerns had thrived for decades, a big change was taking place. The arrival of saloons with monocoque shells – not only from Alfa Romeo, but from Fiat and Lancia – meant that it was no longer practical for them to supply 'rolling chassis'. For a time there was much doom and gloom about the future, until the more forward-looking body-making concerns prepared to modernize themselves. In the end, they and the manufacturers came to a new agreement. Instead of supplying rolling chassis, car-makers would arrange to supply rolling platforms – in effect they would supply part-complete monocoques which comprised already welded underplatform/bulkhead/engine bay pressing assemblies, but these would be without doors, and certainly without any of what we might call the 'super-structure'.

The specialists would then have to come to terms with a steep change in technology. In future they would have to build up special styles from steel, and only steel, and they would have to weld up panels together to the supplied steel underpans as assembly progressed. They would also have to accept that even if their tooling and assembly jigging was simpler than those of the car-maker, they too were now in the business of making monocoque body styles. By definition, they would not be able to cater for so many different cars ever again.

Different Alfa model, different styling house, noticeably different shape, this being Ghia's offering on the basis of the 2000 of 1954.

Look at the nose of this Bertone-styled 1900 Coupé of 1954, and the visual links to the Giulietta Sprint, which was just around the corner.

For those enterprises which were brave, and which could raise the money to retool their businesses, this meant that their output could increase. Those enterprises which would not conform faced death, or at least marginalization as the years progressed.

Almost automatically this meant that coupé styles tended to be visually much closer to those of the saloon cars on which they were based, than ever before. We saw this with coachbuilders' efforts on other makes of car – and soon we would see it on Alfa Romeo 1900 derivatives.

It also meant that the specialist coachbuilders took time to reinvent themselves – by working out how to embrace all-steel welding assembly methods; by raising the money to finance the installation of new tooling; and by choosing which car models to concentrate on.

As far as the 1900 is concerned, this is proven when we consider a few dates. The saloon had been launched, prematurely, in May 1950, and the first technical analyses appeared in October of that year. Only six saloons were actually produced before the end of the year – volume sales began in 1951 – and the first 1900 Sprint coupés and cabriolets (by Touring and Pininfarina, respectively) were not even seen in prototype form until the Geneva Motor Show of March 1951.

Having thought about it very deeply, and after discussing styling trends with their associates, Alfa then decided to supply modified platforms for use in coupé or cabriolet guise, these being arranged to have a shortened wheelbase of 98.4in (2,500mm). This meant that cabins could be more compact, though it would still be possible to provide four-seater (more realistically, two-plus-two) accommodation. In the event, there was a considerable weight saving, the Touring

This was certainly a Bertone and Alfa Romeo 2000, but was different in many ways. More of a 'racing' than a 'road car' treatment, and with a similar front-end theme to several sports-racing Alfas of the same period.

Years after Bertone had shaped the original Giulietta, it produced this much larger two-door four-seater style on the basis of the 2000 model – a style which would also persist on the 2600 until 1966.

From any angle, the 2000's proportions were just as pleasing as those of the smaller Giulietta.

coupé being about 220lb (100kg) lighter than the four-door saloon.

However, in spite of a brave showing in March 1951, and again at Turin in April, the specialists were still not quite ready to deliver cars. Only eight such Sprints (all Touring coupés) were delivered in 1951, series-production did not get underway until 1952, and the very first (and rare) cabriolets were not sold until 1952.

Due to the limits imposed by the basic underbody/front-end coachwork which Alfa Romeo provided, these different Sprints looked virtually identical ahead of the windscreens, and appeared to share the same curved glass. But there was a difference between the two cars, the Touring coupés being more obviously sculpted under the headlamps. Aft of the screen, of course, they were totally different, the Pininfarina cabriolet having a rather ponderously detailed soft-top, while the Touring coupé enjoyed a nicely detailed 'glass-house' with good all-round visibility and the merest suggestion of a rear 'wing' along the rear quarter pressing.

Trends

Although the 1900 Sprints were popular and successful (1,803 two-door coupés would be produced in seven seasons), neither their running gear nor their manufacturer (Touring) had any material influence on what was to follow, for at this stage Bertone was not involved in making production-car body shells for Alfa Romeo.

The true significance of the 1900 Sprints (and from 1954, the 115bhp/1,975cc Super Sprints that succeeded them) was that Touring proved that even in the 1950s, it was still possible to develop an attractive shape on the basis of a rather bland four-door saloon. Even more significant was that this proved that by committing itself to a long production run, and by spending money on fixtures, an independent concern could also make coupé-building of monocoques into a profitable enterprise.

All this was to be invaluable to Alfa Romeo in the future, when the next new-generation model, the Giulietta, came on stream.

2 Giulietta – The Little Beauty

The Giulietta Sprint came into existence in 1954. In so many ways, the car did not have any logical right to succeed. Latter-day product planners would insist that not enough time was given to studying the alternatives. Miracles do happen sometimes, though, and the evolution of the Giulietta was one of them.

From the day it was unveiled at the Turin Motor Show of April 1954, to the day when the last car of all was produced in 1965, Alfa Romeo's Giulietta Sprint was one of the world's most elegant little cars. Aside from the fact that every enthusiast, road tester and customer wanted it to be able to go faster, few had any bad words to say about it. Which, considering that it was an afterthought to a more mundane programme, was remarkable. Its development was not the first phase of a long-term master plan; it was not the culmination of long-term research. In fact, the project was finalized in a great hurry.

Origins

It's always difficult to know where an important industrial story really begins. Is there a 'Eureka' moment when a designer, engineer or planner suddenly realizes what sort of new model is needed? Is it influenced by earlier events, trends and selling experiences? Or is it all bound up in finance, long-term planning and strategy?

As far as the Giulietta project was concerned, it was originally centred around a saloon car, not a coupé, and we have to go back to the late 1940s to see why. Once the Allied bombers had flattened the Portello works in 1943 and 1944, the only way for the Alfa Romeo business to recover was to work immensely hard, and to rely on new financial investment from the Italian state-controlled IRI, on long-term loans from Marshall Aid (from the USA), and on a marketing change of direction which (Alfa hoped) would rake in the profits, and the cash-flow, which the company had previously lacked.

In the late 1940s and early 1950s, Alfa Romeo focused its attention on developing more affordable cars, and selling more of them. This meant restoring the factories to their former glory, and installing new machinery.

The 1900 saloon, launched in 1950, did a great job – it finally jerked Alfa Romeo out of a long-established pre-war/hand-built/luxury mindset, and showed that there was, indeed, life after devastation. However, although the 1900 was built in series, it was never a mass-production model. At its peak in 1953 just 5,411 such cars were built during the year – little more than 100 cars a week – to keep a big and sprawling industrial complex alive.

The 1900's rather leisurely rate of sales was not a result of the car not being good enough (as a comparison, with two ranges in production, Jaguar were making only double the number of sales at the time); it was due to the marketplace for such technologically advanced 2-litre models being rather limited, and the fact that Italian fiscal laws tended to penalize large-engined cars – as they do to this day.

The strategic solution, Alfa concluded, was to try to expand its output, and to do this it was essential to develop a complementary range of cars, still with every recognizable Alfa Romeo feature, but smaller, more affordable, and able to be sold in larger numbers. By definition, every component in such a new car – in particular the

Giulietta Sprint (1954–62, 1964–65)

Layout

Unit-construction body-chassis structure, with steel panels. Two-door, front engine/rear drive, sold as 2+2-seater coupé model.

Engine

Block material	Cast aluminium
Head material	Cast aluminium
Cylinders	4 in-line
Cooling	Water
Bore and stroke	74 × 75mm
Capacity	1,290cc
Main bearings	5
Valves	2 per cylinder, operated by twin-overhead camshafts and inverted bucket-type tappets, driven by chain from crankshaft
Compression ratio	8.0:1 at first, 8.5:1 from late 1958
Carburation	1 downdraught Solex 32 PAIAT

(To 1958):

Max. power	65bhp (net) @ 6,100rpm
Max. torque	80lb ft @ 4,000rpm

(From late 1958):

Max. power	80bhp (net) @ 6,300rpm
Max. torque	72lb ft @ 3,500rpm

Transmission

Four-speed all-synchromesh manual gearbox

Clutch	Single dry plate; hydraulically operated

Internal Gearbox Ratios

(1954–62)

Top	1.00
3rd	1.357
2nd	1.985
1st	3.258
Reverse	3.252
Final drive	4.555:1

(1964–65)

Top	1.00
3rd	1.355
2nd	1.988
1st	3.304
Reverse	3.010
Final drive	4.555:1

Suspension and Steering	
Front	Independent, coil springs, wishbones, anti-roll bar, telescopic dampers
Rear	Live (beam) axle, by coil springs, radius arms, A-bracket, telescopic dampers
Steering	Worm and roller
Tyres	155-15 radial-ply
Wheels	Steel disc, bolt-on
Rim width	4.5in

Brakes	
Type	Drum brakes at front, drums at rear, hydraulically operated (front disc, 1964–65)
Size	10.5 × 2.25in front drums, 10 × 1.75in rear drums
	(10.6in dia. front discs, 1964–65)

Dimensions	
Track	
Front	50.9in (1,292mm)
Rear	50.0in (1,270mm)
Wheelbase	93.7in (2,380mm)
Overall length	156.5in (3,975mm)
Overall width	60.5in (1,537mm)
Overall height	52.0in (1,321mm)
Unladen weight	1,938lb (880kg)

body shell, engine and transmission – would have to be newly developed.

But before development began, there were major problems to be faced. To quote fellow author Richard Bremner: 'Alfa's problem was money, a not unfamiliar difficulty at Portello, and in particular raising enough of it to get a range underway.'

Lottery

Alfa Romeo therefore took a major gamble with their investment in such a car. In 1952 and 1953, after letting it be known that a smaller-engined car was to be put on sale, fund-raising was arranged by organizing and publicizing what was in effect an Italian National Lottery – selling Alfa Romeo debentures. The money would be turned into investment bonds and used as investment seed-corn, with interest to be paid at six-monthly intervals. So far, so conventional.

Yet was there any likelihood of these bonds ever maturing, and the capital being repaid, for at that time no-one could remember how long ago it was that Alfa Romeo had actually made a profit from building cars? Was it *ever* going to be possible to raise the money?

To solve the problem, Alfa resorted to Madison Avenue marketing techniques, inventing a 'Unique Selling Proposition': they would hold a prize draw, which would result in 200 of these debenture holders being awarded a new Giulietta saloon for their support. (At this stage, please note, a Sprint coupé was not even mentioned.)

So the draw was made, 200 lucky prize winners were announced, and every one of them sat complacently back to await delivery. And waited, and waited . . .

The new saloon had been due to meet its public at the Brussels Show at the end of 1953, then at the Geneva Show of March 1954, but both deadlines were missed. The new car was not ready. Anger erupted among the prize winners. There were suspicions of a scam – even though Alfa Romeo was scrupulously honest about the whole thing, this was corruption-ridden Italy, after all – and some suggested that the cars might never be available.

Alfa Romeo, on the other hand, knew precisely what the problem was. Development of the Giulietta saloon car itself had gone ahead quickly and encouragingly enough, but although it was possible to make some of the engines and other running gear, the new tooling, jigging and assembly facilities for the body shell were not complete. In private, the project managers knew that the saloon car could not possibly go on sale until 1955.

So what to do? The solution, as we now know, was to buy time and to find a quick fix. In a tearing hurry, Alfa Romeo approached Bertone of Turin – who was not a regular supplier to Alfa Romeo at this point in time – with a proposal along the following lines: 'We have a problem which we think you can solve. We will provide prototype floorpans of our new small car, we want you to build a sensational-looking coupé, and if the public likes it we guarantee that you will then get a profitable production contract to build more of them. How many? Well, we're not sure. It has to be 200, but we think 500, maybe even 1,000, could eventually be sold. Oh, and by the way, you will have to build the first prototype – a show car – in a matter of weeks, for it *must* go on show at our "home" motor show, Turin, in April 1954, and be ready to start delivering complete shells later in the year . . .'

At this time, Bertone was not one of the Italian coachbuilding industry's biggest players, but it was ambitious. This seemed an unmissable opportunity, even though its factory would have to be equipped to turn out up to twenty shells a week in order to get the 1,000 built within a year. And that was just the start . . .

Even if no rational observer now accepts that Bertone was given only ten days to achieve a miracle with the prototype, there was still an almighty scramble to get a car on show. Bertone did it, however, and the rest is automotive history.

This scramble perhaps explains why the Sprint took shape around the standard-length saloon car wheelbase (ideally it might have been better to choose a shortened wheelbase, but only the standard floorpan was immediately available), and why the new car's styling origins were so diverse. At this stage I should note that the trend-setting shape and equipment which looks so pure, and which has been loved by so many people, was part-Alfa Romeo, part Bertone and part Ghia! How, why, when and where is an arresting tale

---

Bertone – Ace Stylists

Carrozzeria Bertone of Turin was founded in 1912 by Giovanni Bertone, but from the mid-1930s it was his publicity-conscious son Nuccio who became an important personality in the Italian motor industry, and with whom Alfa Romeo was most closely connected.

Between the wars, Bertone's work was done on an individual basis, using virtually no press or folding tools, but wooden formers and individual craftsmanship, though some build contracts for, say, the Lancia Kappa were more substantial.

Bertone's first contact with Alfa Romeo came after the Second World War, when it built coupé and Spider versions of the 6C 2500, and there was huge interest in the series of aerodynamically-shaped 'BAT' coupés which followed in the 1950s. Even so, Bertone was still a small and specialized business in 1954, when Alfa Romeo arranged for the company to build the body shells for the sensational new Giulietta Sprint. This was the beginning of a long and mutually profitable relationship, as contracts then followed for the building of other series-production Alfa Romeos, notably the Giulietta SS Coupé, the 2000 Sprint, the 2600 Sprint and, later, the Montreal, with the style of the Giulia Sprint GT and 1750 saloons (both built entirely by Alfa Romeo) also credited to Bertone.

This coachbuilder, however, was not completely beholden to Alfa Romeo, as its many credits for companies like Ferrari, Fiat, Innocenti, Iso Rivolta, Lamborghini, Lancia, Maserati, NSU, Simca and Volvo make clear. By the 1980s, Bertone's factory at Grugliasco, in the suburbs of Turin, had expanded mightily, and was devoted to long runs of cars such as the Fiat X1/9 and the Fiat Strada Cabriolet, but the company remained independent.

which must wait until the new platform's true significance is detailed.

New Running Gear

So much for the politics, now for the engineering. The new Giulietta, I must re-emphasize, was originally conceived as a four-door saloon car – not a true 'family' car because of its high specification, but a saloon nevertheless. In the short term there was no coupé. The development team, if they could find time, were allowed to build a sporty-looking 'mule', but had not settled on anything by the end of 1953.

In an ideal world, Alfa Romeo would have had their new saloon model tidily and securely on the market before any derivatives. However, as I have already noted, the Sprint appeared first (albeit only in prototype form) because the production-line tooling, jigging, pressing and assembly facilities for this all-new saloon body shell were not ready in time.

The new car, the family of which originally carried the chassis number range of '750' (original derivatives would be 750B for the Sprint, 750C for the Saloon, and 750D for the Pininfarina-styled Spider which followed), was entirely different from the 1900, having a new and more compact platform, a new engine, a new transmission and new suspension components.

The Giulietta was, by any measure, the smallest Alfa Romeo ever to be put on commercial sale, as the following dimensional comparisons make clear:

Feature	Giulietta Saloon	1900
Wheelbase	93.4in	103.5in
	(2,372mm)	(2,628mm)
Overall length	157.1in	173.2in
	(3,990mm)	(4,399mm)
Width	61.0in	63.0in
	(1,549mm)	(1,600mm)
Height	55.1in	58.7in
	(1,399mm)	(1,490mm)
Unladen weight	2,018lb	2,426lb
(four–door)	(915kg)	(1,100kg)

Here was a new car which was not only more than 16in shorter, but more than 400lb lighter than the 1900. Even though the new engine was only a 1.3-litre 'four' which produced a mere 53bhp at first, the Giulietta would be a brisk performer.

Given that they were, in fact, producing their very first small sports saloon, Alfa Romeo really had no previous experience in this area, and few other direct comparisons could even be made within the Italian motor industry. Lancia's new Appia (which had been launched in 1953) was much less powerful and rather smaller, while the Fiat Nuova 1100 (also new in 1953) was a cheap and by no means sporty saloon car.

A series of bold decisions was therefore called for. Led by Dr Ing. Orazio Satta Puliga, the team evolved a compact machine which was, in so many ways, a slimmed-down restatement of the 1900 theme. If they were wrong and the clientele did not buy the cars, then the company would undoubtedly be dragged into insolvency for the last time.

The architecture of the new Giulietta's layout was exactly like that of the 1900, there being a front-mounted engine driving the rear wheels, an all-steel monocoque body shell, a four-cylinder twin-overhead camshaft engine, a four-speed all-synchromesh gearbox, and a beam rear axle. The principles might have been the same but the details were new.

The engine, incidentally, was tipped over slightly towards the left (exhaust) side of the engine bay. This was not done to lower the necessary bonnet height clearance (which it demonstrably did not) but to allow more space on the right side of the engine bay, for bulkier carburettors, aircleaners and airboxes which would follow on later derivatives of the model.

Because the saloon appeared a year after the launch of the beautiful Sprint coupé, the style brought no real surprises. Neat, understated, subtly rounded in so many aspects, yet with the archetypal Alfa grilles and motifs at the front-end, and neatly detailed rear quarters, it looked purposeful and (most importantly for Italian buyers) it made all the right noises.

Although intended to be built in large numbers and for a lengthy period, for products as diverse as the Giulietta saloon, a small delivery van and (eventually) competition cars, the Giulietta's engine was an up-to-the-minute twin-cam design which put every other rival's efforts into the shade. It was unquestionably the most advanced and courageously detailed 1.3-litre power unit of its period; only the 3.4-litre Jaguar XK engine, which was much larger and heavier, could really match it. This apart, a comparison with almost any engine being fitted to any other private car of the day showed that it was forward-looking and had huge potential.

Although it looked similar, in its structure it was totally different to the 1900's power unit (which, of course, would remain in production for some years). It was 1,290cc instead of 1,884cc, with 80 degrees between the line of valves rather than 90 degrees, with an aluminium cylinder head and, this time, an aluminium (instead of a cast-iron) cylinder block. The 1900 was a conventional 'dry-liner' engine, whereas the new Giulietta had slip-fit 'wet' liners.

In its initial form this sturdy five-bearing-crankshaft engine measured 1,290cc, with near-square internal dimensions of a 74mm cylinder bore and a 75mm stroke, and once the drawings that Alfa Romeo released had been studied it was clear that this capacity might eventually be enlarged in future years. In the mid-1950s, however, I doubt if anyone visualized a engine which would eventually be stretched to 1,985cc and 240bhp!

The initial tune was indeed extremely conservative, for in 1955 saloon car form, with a single downdraught Solex carburettor but with only a 7.5:1 compression ratio, it pumped out a mere 53bhp. Even so, the small size of the saloon meant that this was enough to give it a claimed top speed of 87mph.

Behind it was a neatly-detailed four-speed all-synchromesh gearbox. Amazingly for a car of this type, it was originally provided with a steering column gearshift. Even the original Sprint coupés had a column shift; it would be some time (after 7,300 Sprints had been produced) before the more pleasing central control shift was adopted. This gearbox was another important 'building block' in Alfa Romeo's future, and would eventually be redesigned in 1959 to be stronger and to accept a fifth 'overdrive' gear for Giuliettea SS and SZ types, for the final 1300 Sprints, and for all Giulias. The gearbox casing was in aluminium, as was that of the hypoid-bevel rear axle casing.

Independent front suspension was by coil springs, upper and lower wishbones, and with a telescopic damper neatly fitted inside the coil spring itself. At the rear, the live axle was sprung on coil springs (these being positioned partway outboard, on top of the axle tubes themselves), location being assured by a very similar method

---

A-Bracket Suspension Control

In the mid-twentieth century, any motor car chassis designer who was obliged to use a rigid rear axle, tried to locate that axle accurately, his aim being to let it move up and down within precise limits, but not to react against engine torque (by twisting), and not to be allowed to move sideways at all. Many designers used half-elliptic springs to get a 'good enough' result (which it never was), but the more thoughtful ones used coil springs and a series of links to achieve a better compromise.

Over the years, a myriad of methods were tried to achieve the ideal, and Alfa's solution was as elegant as most. First seen in its simplest form under the 1900 model of 1950 was what became known as a pivoting 'A-bracket' linkage, which joined the centre of the axle to the underside of the body. Although rubber bushes allowed *some* flexing, this provided unfettered up and down articulation, but eliminated sideways motion and axle twisting.

A-brackets allied to rigid axles were used in a number of distinguished cars – the Ford Lotus-Cortina, for example – but it was under every Giulietta and (in refined form) under every Giulia, except the TZ, that it became so effective.

Why 'A-bracket'? Simply because, in plan view, the bracket had the profile of a broad 'A', the apex of which was fixed to the axle.

to that of the 1900 – long, forward-facing tubular radius arms closely tucked in alongside the tyre/wheel positions, and a tubular A-bracket which linked the top of the axle casing precisely to the underside of the body shell itself.

Coupé Style

Although everyone gasped at the sheer elegance of the 2+2 fixed-head coupé style which Bertone put on display at the Turin Motor Show, this had neither been conceived instantly, nor without pain. In the beginning, even in 1952, Alfa Romeo had started sketching up coupés to add to this new Giulietta range, and well before the end of 1953 a running prototype of sorts was being tested.

It was a start – but no more than that. Bertone, once given the helter-skelter challenge, set its Chief Designer Franco Scaglione to develop an elegant derivative, and at the same time Alfa also brought in further help from Felice Mario Boano, who was currently working with Carrozzeria Ghia. It was an instant recipe for conflict, which Alfa Romeo, in true Italian 'fix-it' mode, attempted to defuse elegantly. Although the Bertone style was preferred, it was agreed that Ghia (whose factory facilities were much superior at this time) should help to build the prototypes themselves.

That was the original deal, but too many artistic feathers had been ruffled, the result being that Boano and Ghia eventually walked away from the project. Neither would work again for Alfa Romeo – Boano would eventually find a secure and well-respected home running the entire Fiat in-house styling studios – and Bertone sweated blood to complete the first car itself.

The result was an artistic triumph. Even though, as stated, the two-door coupé ran on what was intended to be the four-door saloon car's platform and wheelbase, this was a beautifully detailed, low and sleek 2+2-seater machine.

In many ways it had been influenced by the 1900 Sprint from Carrozzeria Touring (who were not asked to produce the Giulietta Sprint prototype, presumably because they were already fully occupied), for the front-ends were very similar, the proportions could be compared directly, the window cut-lines certainly related to each other, and both had that seductive sloping tail. Yet the new Bertone-styled Giulietta Sprint was one on its own. Not a line was out of place – there was not even a suggestion of excess brightwork; it was a car which looked right (magnificently right!) from any angle, including the overhead view.

In fact, the prototype was different from later production cars in two obvious details. Firstly, there was an external fuel filler cap on the right rear quarter (it would be relocated to the boot on production cars), and secondly – and more significantly, in view of 1960s trends – there was a fully-fledged lift-up hatchback panel surrounding the rear window glass: when the car eventually went on sale, it would have become a conventional coupé with an opening boot lid.

The interior was simply equipped, not to say stark, and was laid out initially as a two-seater, with space behind the seats being allocated for luggage stowage (or optional clip-on cushions). Media outlets of the day noted the steering column gearchange, but were too polite to criticize it.

The original engine tune was relatively modest, though even the initial 65bhp was significantly better than that proposed for the saloon version. A more highly tuned 80bhp derivative would not follow until mid-1958, and would then be standardized. Under the skin, the running gear was almost pure (still-secret) Giulietta saloon, and it is worth noting that *The Motor's* supposedly authoritative Technical Editor Laurence Pomeroy got one detail most hilariously wrong, for he stated that the rear suspension was by variable-rate leaf springs. Odd that, for Alfa never used leaf springs in any of its post-war cars.

On Sale At Last

Having shown the Sprint in Turin, Alfa Romeo had gained some breathing space. Although they were not ready to start delivering cars – Bertone had not installed any press-tool capability to allow them to build all-steel body shells, and Alfa

Romeo itself was barely ready to start manufacturing engines and transmissions – this at least allowed them to placate their Lottery winners.

Even so, the production contract still had to be settled, and Bertone still had to honour its intentions. In the spring and summer of 1954, with the media champing at the bit to be allowed to try cars, and with the line of customers getting ever longer, the car was readied.

First of all, Bertone retouched the car, giving it a conventional fixed rear window and an upward-opening boot lid, and at the same time re-equipped its downtown Turin premises to build the shells in quantity. Although Bertone had previously built shells in numbers – the Arnolt-MG and Arnolt-Bristols being a case in point – much of their previous output had been one-off styles and competition shells, including those astonishing 'BAT' aerodynamic studies for Alfa Romeo. Up to that point, they had not build monocoque shells in series, or in numbers.

All this changed in the autumn of 1954, when a trickle of bodies were completed in Turin, trucked north-east up the autostrada to Portello, and haltingly converted into cars by Alfa Romeo. The records show that only twelve cars were produced before the end of 1954, but by this time many more were already on the way. In 1955 no fewer than 1,415 Sprints would follow (this being the year in which the saloon, for which Alfa Romeo produced its own shells, also went on the market), 2,107 in 1956 and 2,573 in 1957.

Yet because the sporty market all over the world was more restricted than that of the saloon, even these achievements were swamped by demand for the saloons, of which 6,348 were produced in 1956 and 8,939 in 1957.

Alfa Romeo, it seemed, had made all the right decisions about their future strategy, for the Giulietta family formed the foundation for a whole series of fine cars that followed. One of the elements that contributed to this success was that

The all-new Giulietta saloon, which appeared in 1955, was launched after the Giulietta Sprint, though it was the fastest-selling derivative, which made the Sprint, and of course the Spider, economically viable.

From side-on there was little to link the Giulietta saloon with the sleeker, lower and much more sporty Sprint. Yet the two cars shared the same platform, wheelbase, track dimensions and running gear.

Bertone's shaping of the original Giulietta Sprint was sheer genius. By the standards of the day – it was unveiled in 1954 – it was peerless. This was the original 'Lottery' prototype, complete with hatchback. Except for the deletion of the prototype hatchback, the Giulietta Sprint looked exactly the same when finally built in 1965.

(above) *This was the very first Giulietta Sprint, as displayed at the Turin Motor Show in April 1954, when the theme of the coupé included a hatchback rather than a conventional rear window and boot lid. It was a premature launch, as only twelve cars would be delivered to customers before the end of the year.*

Even when it was only a single hand-crafted prototype with a hatchback, Bertone's Giulietta Sprint had almost every other detail of the legendary car that would charm tens of thousands.

the little car had taken off in the USA, the cash-rich continent which was already learning to love other European sports cars, such as Triumph's TR2 and the MGA. Early Sprints arrived on America's East Coast priced at $4,070 (£1,453), which buyers thought very reasonable.

Although by modern standards the earlier Sprints were not outstandingly fast (the 65bhp cars struggled to reach 100mph (160kph), and 0–60mph acceleration took more than fifteen seconds), they were brisk by the standards of the 1950s. Not only that, but this was done with supple suspension as opposed to a bone-jarring ride (those who complained that a Sprint rolled too much usually did not realize that these cars hung on tenaciously until very high cornering speeds were reached), and with great panache. Only those with a heart of stone, and a tin ear, could drive off in a Sprint, and fail to rev it up towards the 6,100rpm peak and enjoy all the built-in sensations.

As the United States' *Motor Trend* magazine wrote in October 1956:

Give the Alfa Romeo Giulietta the right place to be driven hard, where it can be pushed through corners as fast as *you* dare to go, and it will get you there quicker and safer than most cars with four times the horsepower. To appreciate this Italian engineering masterpiece from Milan, you would want to drive it hard on curving byways, and not pussyfoot your way among the behemoths on Main Street, USA. It's only where you can stuff your foot in it, revving the engine to between 4,000 and its maximum of 6,000, that you can wring out its best performance ...

And that was the point of the Sprint – it was a car which not only invited every driver to push hard, but which had already been engineered with such treatment in mind.

Themes and Variations

Looking ahead from 1955, though, not even Alfa Romeo's top bosses could have realized how this range was going to expand, improve and influence the birth of other such fine Alfas, for many of the excellent cars that followed were not con-

This was the charmingly detailed nose of the original Giulietta Sprint of 1954, with the established 'shield-shaped' grille as its centrepiece. In the next ten years, the only changes would be to the decoration of the auxiliary grilles.

Would you, Mr Stylist, find any way of improving on this exquisite shape, if you had been asked to look at it again in the mid-1950s? No? Thought not . . .

sidered until the end of the 1950s. Even if I confine myself to a listing of the 1,290cc derivatives (for the 1,570cc Giulia of 1962 onwards would dwarf every earlier Giulietta achievement), there is still a formidable line-up:

- Giulietta saloons eventually enjoyed 74bhp: well over 100,000 were produced.
- The Pininfarina-styled Spiders were mechanically identical to the equivalent Sprints: 17,096 were produced from 1955 to 1962.

- The Sprint Veloce arrived in 1956, at once more powerful yet lighter than the Sprint: 3,058 of these were produced.
- Bertone produced its own super-special and rebodied Sprint Speciale types: 1,366 were produced between 1957 and 1962.
- Zagato produced the magnificent, lightweight Sprint Zagato (SZ) from 1960 to 1962. Only 210 were ever produced, but what a difference they made to the marque's reputation.

This was the Giulietta Sprint's facia/instrument panel layout, as first seen in the mid-1950s. Those were the days when customers were happy with a direct rather than a remote-control gearchange, and, amazingly, with an awful umbrella-handled handbrake.

By the end of the 1950s, the Giulietta Sprint had been given a slightly different front grille (mesh instead of a stripe on the auxiliary grilles), and badging on the front wings.

Along the way, there would be regular improvements, and updating of an already advanced specification. And even then, in the early 1960s, this was not the end of the story, for there would also be 1,570cc-engined versions of the same cars to add to the list.

Pininfarina's Spider

Although Pininfarina's curvaceous little two-seater was a masterpiece, it was not a closed coupé, therefore I have only space to summarize it here.

Pininfarina – the Styling House

For many years Pininfarina has been one of the most famous coachbuilding 'names' in the world. Battista Farina (no 'Pinin' at that stage) joined his brother's Stabilimenti Farina (of Turin) in the 1920s. The company produced a number of special bodies for Alfa Romeo in the 1930s, but it was not until the 1940s that the company's 'line' became so famous, and that its ability to manufacture cars in reasonable numbers became obvious.

First with the Lancia Aurelia B20 Coupé, and then with the Alfa Romeo Giulietta Spider, the company cemented its reputation. At the time, its artistic abilities were sold around the world, notably to companies like Peugeot in France, and to the British Motor Corporation in the UK.

Expansion – both in styling studies and in factory space – was brisk in the 1960s, and before long, Pininfarina became capable of building thousands of body shells every year. In this way – and especially in its work on the Giulietta Spider, then the Giulia-based 1600/Duetto – it became one of Alfa Romeo's contractors of choice. Although Ferrari was one of its most high-profile clients, there was always much to do for Alfa Romeo.

Still independent to this day, Pininfarina is one of the top-ranking styling houses. Alfa Romeo was clever enough to spot this many years ago, and has never lost touch.

Evolved less than a year after the original Sprint had appeared, it made its first appearance in 1955. Based on a shortened-wheelbase version of the Giulietta platform – 88.6in (2,250mm) instead of the 93.7in (2,380mm) of the Sprint – with only two seats and a fold-back soft-top, the body shell of this car was always produced at the Pininfarina factory in Turin. From this time, therefore, Alfa-watchers at the side of the Turin–Milan autostrada could see two types of transporters with Pininfarina (Spider) and Bertone (Sprint) body shells on the way to Portello.

Sprint Veloce – More Sport, More Power

In 1956 Alfa made a more serious attempt to provide a new Sprint that could be used in motorsport. Because of the Sprint's monocoque body-chassis construction, they were not able to lighten the car by much, but by boosting the engine's performance and by stripping out some of the 'creature comforts' they could give a new version of the car – the Sprint Veloce – a better potential.

The big change was to the 1,290cc engine. At this time the Sprint was still only available with the 65bhp engine, so when Alfa was able to rate

---

The Spider

Although this book concentrates on coupés, we must never forget the Spiders which ran side by side with the Giuliettas and Giulias throughout their lives. Indeed, thousands of enthusiasts preferred their Alfa Romeos with fold-back soft-tops and with only two seats.

The Giulietta Spider, styled by Pininfarina, who also produced all the body shells, used the same basic platform but had a completely different structure. The wheelbase was cropped from 93.7in (2,380mm) to 88.6in (2,250mm), and though the nose looked similar, the shape was unique.

However, for every Sprint, there was a mechanically equivalent Spider, with 80bhp and 90bhp 1,290cc engines, and (from 1962) five-speed 92bhp and 112bhp 1,570cc Giulia-sized engines. All in all, there were 27,437 Pininfarina-manufactured Spiders; purely because they are open-top cars, they are somehow seen as more glamorous today.

Throughout its career, the Pininfarina Spider tracked the Sprint, sharing the same engine/transmission/suspension layouts, but because it was always a little lighter – say 1,896lb (860kg) instead of 1,940lb (880kg) for mid-1950s examples – and smaller, it was just faster and maybe more 'chuckable' than the Sprint, though the body shell itself was by no means as torsionally strong as that of the Sprint.

Early Spiders had 80bhp, Spider Veloce types had 90bhp, while the later Giulia-engined types had 112bhp.

Giulietta Sprint Veloce (1956–62)

As for Giulietta Sprint, except for:

Compression ratio: 9.1:1; two horizontal Weber 40DCOE3 carburettors; 90bhp @ 6,500rpm, 87lb ft @ 4,500rpm; final drive 4.1:1; unladen weight 1,973lb (895kg).

the Sprint Veloce at 90bhp at 6,500rpm, this was a remarkable improvement – no less than 38 per cent in peak power, in fact. This was the result of a novel fuelling system: two of the new-type twin-choke Weber 40DCOE3 carburettors, a 9.0:1 compression ratio and revised camshaft timing with 64 degrees of 'overlap' around Top Dead Centre. The carburettors were so relatively bulky (as was the cool-air trunking that accompanied them) that Alfa's original decision to cant

The Giulietta Sprint Veloce was introduced in 1956. The most important improvement on the Sprint was that the SV was fitted with a 90bhp instead of an 80bhp engine – but the price was considerably higher.

Without help from the badges on the front wings – which not only spelt out 'Sprint Veloce' but included the 'B' (for Bertone) emblem – it would not be possible to tell the more powerful type from the original.

the engine over towards the exhaust side was immediately justified. All this, along with a sturdy centre floor gearchange, made the latest Sprint Veloce into a more purposeful machine.

More important was the way that weight was stripped out – on the early versions at least. These were provided with plastic sliding windows in the doors and a reduced level of trim and fittings, the car being intended as a serious motorsport two-seater coupé. Early cars, too, used aluminium pressings for the bonnet, boot lid and door skins. It was originally claimed that up to 221lb (100kg) had been saved.

Naturally, this specialization came at a price – 1,735,000 Italian lira for the Sprint, compared with 2,050,000 lira for the Sprint Veloce – but hundreds of customers were happy to pay up. Yet sales were rather limited, not necessarily due to low demand, but because of Alfa's and Bertone's own abilities to produce. In the first full sales year, 1957, for example, 458 Sprint Veloces were produced, compared with 2,115 Sprints – the SV making up just 18 per cent of the total of cars with this body style. There was, however, no doubt that this was a much quicker car than the Sprint, as early class success in the Mille Miglia proved, the untuned road cars having a top speed of 112mph (180kph).

Exports began almost at once, but the specification of the normal-production road cars soon changed, with a reversion to normal steel pressings, to conventional wind-up glass windows, and to a smartly-trimmed interior. Alfa's own historic records now credit the Sprint Veloce with being 33lb (15kg) heavier than the original Sprint, which does not accord with how the cars had raced at first!

From mid-1959, and along with other models in the Giulietta range, the Sprint Veloce progressed from the '750' chassis number range to the '101' range, and although this was done without any change to the style or general layout of the cars, the major improvement seems to have been to the internals of the engine (maybe preparation for a larger 1.6-litre power unit had to be considered) and the fitment of a stronger type of four-speed gearbox, complete with Porsche-type

synchromesh; it was this box that would eventually grow up to become a five-speeder in the Giulia and related models.

Writing in *Autosport* in March 1959, Technical Editor John Bolster enthused over a Sprint Veloce (in standard tune) which he borrowed from club racing driver Richard Shepherd-Barron. This was one of the later types, complete with wind-up windows and normal steel coachwork. Bolster, whose tests reflected that he always liked to think the best of any car he drove, was clearly bowled over by the Sprint Veloce:

> There are certain cars which are acknowledged throughout the motor sporting world as being thoroughbreds, and among these the Alfa Romeo Giulietta stands very high… if a poll of the readers of *Autosport* were undertaken, the Sprint Veloce version would be voted just about the most desirable car that money can buy… This Alfa Romeo is thus a small car of immense technical interest. When I took my seat, I found that entry was easy, and that the all-round visibility is excellent, aided by the deletion of triangular ventilating panels from the front windows. The rear windows may be opened slightly outwards to give a draught-free extractor effect. The driving position is very 'Dr Farina'… The Alfa handles particularly well, especially on wet roads. The cornering power is very high, and one gets a splendid feeling of being truly in command of the little machine. There is a certain amount of roll, but this is scarcely noticed from inside the car. The suspension, steering and roadholding are all of a very high standard…

It was, in other words, the sort of car that John Bolster thought had no match in the UK. On the other hand, it was expensive. With all British taxes paid, the 1959 Sprint Veloce retailed at £2,698, which compared with only £1,266 for the MGA Twin-Cam (of similar performance), and £1,764 for a Jaguar XK150 Fixed-Head Coupé.

Maturity – and a 1600 Version

By the start of the 1960s, the Giulietta range had matured completely, for saloons, coupés and Spiders were being sold in great profusion. Not only that, but the utterly different Romeo range of light vans (which, unlikely as it sounds, were powered by the twin-cam engine) had also made their mark.

The basic platform was so successful, and so obviously sporting, that Alfa Romeo had also encouraged Bertone and Zagato to do their own thing, the result being that the independents created the Sprint Speciale (SS) and the Sprint Zagato (SZ) types (*see* Chapter 3).

The definitive Sprint, slightly facelifted in 1959 with a retouched front end, with its internally stronger engine and more sturdy gearbox, had also enjoyed 80bhp since 1958, and was an excellent all-round car. Sales of 5,558 in 1960 and 4,962 in 1961 proved this. All of this was reflected in what *Road & Track* magazine had to say about the car in 1961. Their problem, at first, concerned the style, for:

> The styling of the Sprint . . . is so devoid of frills that it leaves one a trifle short of descriptive material. There are no fins, chromed spears or sculpturing – just smooth flowing lines . . . For a car of such small overall dimensions, the Sprint has a marvellous amount of usable room inside. In fact it is available as a four-seater (which our test car was) and, although the rear seats are hardly spacious, four people can actually be transported about in the car.

Road & Track, like so many other publications, was so taken by this car that it found itself tempted to lay on the praise too thickly. It was not surprising that the article's final sentence was: 'Add to this the panel-fit and the general finish of the various appointments and you have what is for many a nearly irresistible automobile.'

But time was running out for the Giulietta Sprint and Sprint Veloce models, not because they were no longer saleable, but because they were soon to be replaced by larger-engined types. In June 1962 Alfa Romeo unveiled their latest large-investment project: a new, square-rig saloon model called Giulia, which was intended to complement, not replace, the Giulietta saloon.

The new car featured a 1.6-litre version of the Giulietta engine and a five-speed gearbox, both of which were developed from those already being used in the Giuliettas and Giulietta SS/SZ types, respectively. At the same time – actually at the same press conference – another pair of new models were announced, titled Giulia 1600 Sprint and the Giulia 1600 Spider. This was the point at which the Giulietta Sprint Veloce was dropped.

The new model names tell their own story, for they were well-established cars which had been given new running gear, and modified

No sooner had Alfa Romeo revealed the larger Giulia model than the Sprint was upgraded, giving it the more torquey 92bhp / 1,570cc engine and its five-speed gearbox. Thus retitled Giulia 1600 Sprint, it was made from 1962 to 1964.

Except in detail decoration, the Giulia Sprint of 1962–64 carried the same facia and instrument display as that of earlier types.

The Giulia Sprint of 1962–64 could be distinguished from the earlier Giulietta Sprint by the '1600' badges on the front wings.

From 1962 to 1964 the 1.6-litre-engined Giulia Sprint (the final derivative of the Giulietta) had '1600' badges on the front wings and on the boot lid. By this time, too, the stop-/tail lamp clusters had been enlarged.

accordingly. Detailed analysis of these new engine and transmission 'building blocks' can be found in Chapter 4. However, as far as the new Giulia 1600 Sprint of 1962–64 was concerned, the basic updates were as follows:

Feature	Giulia 1600 Sprint	Giulietta Sprint
Body shell/ style	Two-door 2+ 2 seat, 1600 badge on flanks and tail	Same basic style, no badges
Engine	92bhp/1,570cc	80bhp/1,290cc
Gearbox	Five-speed	Four-speed
Final drive	5.125:1	4.555:1
Brakes	Front drum/ rear drum (front discs on later versions)	Front drum/ rear drum

The 'new' car, in other words, was really a thorough rework of the well-loved Giulietta Sprint, but with a 'Giulia transplant' of engine and gearbox.

Visually, from the outside the only update was that discreet '1600' badges were fitted to the front wings (behind the front wheel cutouts) and to the boot lid itself, though there was little difference to the interior, for which the rear seat cushions were still optional extras. The 1.6-litre engine had a slightly deeper cylinder block, the better to accommodate an 82mm stroke, but for the Sprint the 92bhp peak output (positively sober compared with the 100bhp of the white-hot 1.3-litre SS/SZ types of a couple of years earlier) was achieved by using only a single dual-choke downdraught Solex carburettor.

The ratios inside the five-speed gearbox were the same as those of the new Giulia saloon, but much 'wider' than those used in the ultra-sporting SS/SZ types. Because fourth gear was direct, and fifth gear was an 'overdrive' ratio, this meant that the final drive ratio of the new car was numerically higher than before.

Five-Speed Gearboxes – Alfa Pioneers

Nowadays even the most humble shopping car tends to have a five-speed gearbox, and the true Supercars often offer six speeds, but when the Giuliettas came along in the 1950s they were distinct rarities.

How many forward gears should a car have? That depends on what speed range is involved, and also on what sort of torque delivery comes out of the engine. In the 1930s, many cars (most American cars, in fact) managed very well on three speeds, European Fords would consider nothing else until the 1950s, by which time any car with sporty pretensions found a four-speed box perfectly satisfactory.

Alfa Romeo settled on four speeds in the 1930s, and even the famous Tipo 158/159 Grand Prix cars of the 1940s were four-speed. Then came the breakthrough. First with the special-bodied Giulietta SS (the first cars built in 1957), and shortly afterwards with the bigger 2000 saloons (which entered production in 1957–58), Alfa Romeo offered five-speed gearboxes as standard.

This was a world first. Alpine-Renault had sold a few five-speed A106s, really racing sports cars, but there was no other competition. The British were evolving four-speed plus a separate overdrive control, but that didn't really count.

It was yet another novelty, therefore, of which Alfa Romeo could be justly proud. It was pragmatic, too: whereas five-speeders were confined to the ultra-sporting Giuliettas and the 2000 at first, from 1962 (and the arrival of the new-generation Giulia) they became mass-production fittings.

As tested by *Autocar* in 1963, the 1600 Sprint proved to be faster than the 1.3-litre/80bhp Sprint, but not sensationally so. Top speed was 108mph (173kph) (not as high, seemingly, as the Giulietta Sprint Veloce, perhaps because of the lower overall gearing), though this 2,142lb

In a happy change of mind, Alfa Romeo, who had dropped the Giulietta Sprint in favour of the Giulia Sprint in 1962, revived the original car from 1964 to 1965, this time calling it the 1300 Sprint and fitting '1300' badges.

(972kg) now sprinted up to 60mph in 13.2 seconds.

1300 Sprint Reborn

Within a year of replacing the original Giulietta Sprint with the Giulia 1600 Sprint derivative, Alfa Romeo realized that they had made a mistake. Some potential clients did not like the idea of a 1.6-litre-engined car, and there was still a demand – although not enormous – for the old 1.3-litre version to remain on sale.

Adept by now at playing the 'mix-and-match' game, Alfa Romeo reacted quickly. Before the end of 1963 a final-final derivative, named '1300 Sprint', had appeared. This, in effect, was no more than a very slightly modified Giulietta Sprint, still with the 80bhp/1.3-litre, and still with the four-speed gearbox, but with the latest type of facia panel display, and with front disc brakes. Like the Giulia 1600 Sprint, these cars had engine-size badges on the flanks and the tail – '1300' in this case.

Not a high-selling car, nor ever meant to be so,

it held the fort at the entry-level of this market sector, but died away in 1965, the very last of this sporting family to be produced. The word 'stop gap' was sometimes applied to these final cars, but Alfa Romeo eventually shrugged off such criticism by quoting the following production figures:

Year	Giulietta Sprint	Giulietta Sprint Veloce	Giulia 1600 Sprint	Giulietta 1300 Sprint
1960	5,558	539	–	–
1961	4,962	884	–	–
1962	1,157	261	3,702	–
1963	–	–	3,388	289
1964	–	–	17	1,282
1965	–	–	–	329

By 1965, the modern generation of Giulia Sprint GTs had arrived, and were selling extremely well. The future, as far as Alfa Romeo was concerned, lay in larger-engined, more spacious, permanent 2+2-seater coupés – and once again Bertone provided the style.

3 Sprint Speciale and Sprint Zagato

By 1957, one might have imagined that Bertone would have been happy to carry on producing body shells for the Giulietta Sprint, raking in the proceeds, and not even contemplating taking on other worries or problems. But this was Italy, the country where high-performance cars are a passion, a religion, an obsession, even. Which explains why the Turin-based styling house astonished the world with a further, sleeker and altogether more ambitious variation on the theme at the 1957 Turin Motor Show – the first prototype of which became the Sprint Speciale.

And these were not Bertone's first thoughts on the matter, for many artistically minded observers linked the new SS to a rather different 1956 project car which Bertone had called the Alfa Sportiva. It seemed Chief Designer Franco Scaglione had been busy.

So where did the new Sprint Speciale fit into the scheme of things? Only peripherally, it seems, as far as Alfa Romeo was concerned, though as Bertone would be taking the commercial risk in shaping a new coupé and arranging to have the monocoques built in series, Alfa Romeo was prepared to indulge what was fast becoming its favourite styling house by assembling and marketing the complete cars.

SS – So Many Differences

Like so many derivative Alfa Romeos, before and since, the Sprint Speciale was at the same time so similar to and so different from related products. The first thing to note was that it was not a new car built on the same platform as the Giulietta Sprint, but took shape on the shorter (yet related) platform of the Giulietta Spider. But wasn't it Pininfarina that normally worked on that short platform … ?

No matter. Alfa Romeo, who in any case supplied these platforms to its chosen styling houses, could easily cope with such complications, and prepared to do so. Bertone, for its part, elected to produce a two-seater closed car (the Sprint was an optional 2+2 seater), the theory being that it would be the most streamlined variety possible.

As originally shown at Turin in October 1957 – and titled Sprint Spinta – here was a car that must, surely, have been evolved with motorsport in mind. The prototype was not only clad in light aluminium, and had plastic side and rear windows, but also had the very minimum of interior trim. Mentioned too, though not detailed at the time, was the fact that there was a 100bhp version of the already-famous twin-cam 1,290cc engine up front, and that this would be the very first small-engined Alfa Romeo to be fitted with a five-speed transmission.

It all sounded very promising, yet, at the same time, here was a shape that was somehow more style than substance, even though Bertone's recent credentials included the shaping of the sensational BAT5 and BAT7 project cars.

Although the general proportions of the cabin and the shell itself were as they would be on the series-production cars that followed in 1959, if this was a potential competition car, why was it carrying so much overhang at front and rear (for overhang equals weight), and why were there some obvious decorative touches which no competition car needed?

Interestingly, the nose of the prototype was

Giulietta Sprint Speciale/Giulia Sprint Speciale (1957–62, 1963–65)

Layout

Unit-construction body-chassis structure, with steel and aluminium panels. Two-door, front engine/rear drive, sold as two-seater coupé model.

Engine

Block material	Cast aluminium
Head material	Cast aluminium
Cylinders	4 in-line
Cooling	Water
Bore and stroke	74 × 75mm
Capacity	1,290cc
Main bearings	5
Valves	2 per cylinder, operated by twin-overhead camshafts and inverted bucket-type tappets, driven by chain from crankshaft.

Giulietta type, 1,290cc: bore and stroke 74 × 75mm; compression ratio 9.7:1; two horizontal twin-choke Weber 40DCO3 carburettors; 100bhp @ 6,500rpm, 85lb ft @ 4,000rpm.

Giulia type, 1,570cc (SS only): bore and stroke 78 × 82mm; compression ratio 9.7:1; two horizontal twin-choke Weber DCOE 2 carburettors; 112bhp (DIN) @ 6,200rpm, 98lb ft @ 4,200rpm.

Transmission

Five-speed all-synchromesh manual gearbox

Clutch	Single dry plate; hydraulically operated

Internal Gearbox Ratios

	Giulietta	Giulia
Top	0.854	0.791
4th	1.00	1.00
3rd	1.357	1.355
2nd	1.985	1.988
1st	3.258	3.304
Reverse	3.252	3.010
Final drive	4.555:1	4.555:1

Suspension and Steering

Front	Independent, coil springs, wishbones, anti-roll bar, telescopic dampers
Rear	Live (beam) axle, by coil springs, radius arms, A-bracket, telescopic dampers
Steering	Worm and roller
Tyres	155-15 radial-ply
Wheels	Steel disc, bolt-on
Rim width	4.5in

Brakes

Type	Drum brakes at front, drums at rear, hydraulically operated (front disc, 1963–65)
Size	10.5 × 2.25in front drums, 10 × 1.75in rear drums
	(10.6in dia. front discs, 1963–65)

Giulietta Sprint Speciale/Giulia Sprint Speciale (1957–62, 1963–65) *continued*

Dimensions

Track	
Front	50.9in (1,292mm)
Rear	50.0in (1,270mm)
Wheelbase	88.6in (2,250mm)
Overall length	166.9in (4,240mm)
Overall width	65.6in (1,665mm)
Overall height	47.6in (1,210mm)
Unladen weight	(Giulietta SS) 1,896lb (860kg)
	(Giulia SS) 2,095lb (950kg)

Bertone's Sprint Speciale was the third type of sporting car to appear on the same platform. Announced in 1957, it had a shorter wheelbase, a 100bhp version of the already famous 1,290cc engine, and along with the SZ was the first to use a five-speed gearbox. It would remain in production until 1966, with a 1.6-litre Giulia engine (as used in this particular car) fitted from 1963.

A nose-on view of the Giulietta Sprint Speciale, which was effectively Bertone's second 'take' on the idea of a coupé shape for this model. Under the skin the platform was like that of the familiar Sprint, but with a more powerful engine and a five-speed gearbox.

The Bertone-shaped – and constructed – Giulietta Sprint Speciale of 1957 had a sleek and differently proportioned coupé style, which incorporated this sharply cut-off tail panel.

The Giulietta Sprint Speciale, by Bertone, had a completely different body from that of the Sprint, on whose platform it was based, for there was not a single shared

Look at this study of the Giulietta Sprint Speciale of 1957, by Bertone, then look again. Are there any styling clues to other cars of the day: a touch of Mercedes-Benz 300SL around the nose and front wheelarch flares, perhaps? Otherwise it is unmistakably unique.

very low, and at this stage carried no Alfa Romeo shield, while the frontal area had been reduced so far that Alfa was claiming a top speed of at least 120mph (193kph). To quote *The Motor's* rather breathless description:

The front end offers an exceptionally smart penetration through the air and the rake of the windscreen is altogether exceptional: of the order of 30 degrees. Standing only four feet high, the tail sweeps away on a regular radius, so that there is a large platform

beneath the rear window for the carriage of miscella-
neous objects as well as substantial luggage space
behind the individual seats.

Autocar noted all this, and also pointed out that:
'as there are no front bumpers and only light ones
at the rear, it would be rather prone to minor
damage when parking.'

This was, nevertheless, an astonishing new
style, and both Alfa Romeo and Bertone made it
clear that it would soon start to sell replicas.
However, Alfa's records show that only five cars
were built in 1957 – all of them, I am sure, prototype and development cars – for there would
be big changes before series-production machinery began to filter out in 1959.

Series-production SS types still looked startling by current standards, but were somewhat
less specialized than the prototypes and early
'homologation' cars had been. Importantly, Alfa
Romeo and Bertone eventually seem to have
abandoned all thoughts of using such cars in
motorsport (the smaller, lighter and more purposeful Zagato-inspired SZ was already evolving
behind closed doors in 1957), which explains
why (after a short initial run of 100 lightweights
to gain Group 3 sporting homologation) the
monocoque body shells were built entirely out of
pressed-steel sheet, for except for the boot lid
itself, aluminium no longer figured. Soon after
this the line of the nose was raised a little, which
allowed adequate cooling air to get to the engine
bay in low-speed driving.

The style of the production-ready car was subtly but definitely changed too, for Bertone had
been encouraged to add a conventional Alfa
Romeo shield in the centre of the grille, and
though the nose was still very low, side lamps had
somehow been squeezed into the shell below the
headlamps, and a rather curvaceous but distinctly flimsy-looking chrome front bumper had also
been added.

It was at the rear that the major change took
place. The prototype had featured a long rear
window glass, a boot lid whose corners were
pushed forward on each side of that backlight
glass, and a neatly rounded-off tail. Production

cars, on the other hand, were treated to a sharply
cut-off tail treatment (this pre-dated what Mich-
elotti would do for Triumph at the end of the
1960s, and what Pininfarina would do for the
'Mk II' Alfa Duetto Spider at about the same
time), while the opening boot lid was reshaped
with a more conventional cutout shape, its rear
edge actually overhanging the new cut-off panel
feature.

The result of this 'softening' of the Sprint Speciale's specification was that the weight of the car
shot up, an evolution that would, in any case, have
made it less competitive in motorsport.

But was it critical? Here, as justification, is a
comparison of unladen weights between the four
important coupé derivatives of the 1.3-litre
Giulietta family:

Giulietta Type	Unladen Weight	Power/ Weight Ratio
Sprint (65bhp)	1,940lb (880kg)	75bhp/ton
Sprint Veloce	1,973lb (895kg)	100bhp/ton
Sprint Speciale (road car)	1,896lb (860kg)	118bhp/ton
SZ Zagato	1,731lb (785kg)	129bhp/ton

So, even with the same weight of fuel and driver
on board, the SS was immediately rendered
uncompetitive by the tiny SZ which was soon to
follow.

Remarkable Power Unit

The main attraction of the original Sprint Speciale was hidden away, however, for this was the
very first car in the Giulietta family to get an
extremely powerful 100bhp version of the
1,290cc engine, along with the '101-Series' 'overdrive' five-speed gearbox.

This small twin-cam power unit had already
proved to be remarkably tuneable. Even though
all the fundamentals suggested that it could be so
– twin-overhead camshafts, part-spherical combustion chambers, nicely detailed inlet and
exhaust ports, and the use of a short stroke which
allowed it to rev freely – over the years it continued to amaze everyone who worked on it.

Independent tuners, notably Conrero, had already managed to expand it to nearly 1.5 litres, and it was companies like this that fed their hard-won, race-proven findings back to Milan, where more and more 'goodies' could then be developed.

Originally launched with 65bhp in the Giulietta Sprint, this was a power unit that looked good, but was developing only 50bhp/litre. Alfa Romeo, though, was peopled with enthusiasts and experienced race engineers whose talents had already produced magnificent post-war cars like the all-conquering 158/159 Grand Prix cars, so they already knew how to improve on the original.

For the period, the engine tune of the Sprint Speciale – 100bhp at 6,500rpm – was quite exceptional, for there were no other series-production road cars which could approach such a day-in, day-out rating of 77bhp/litre. By comparison, even the virtually hand-built Ferrari 250GT of the period was rated at 81bhp/litre (and that was really a racing V12), while Europe's other mainstream 'twin-cam' car, the Jaguar XK150, was rated at only 62bhp/litre.

Moving up from 65bhp (original Sprint) to 90bhp (Sprint Veloce) and then on to 100bhp (Sprint Speciale) in only three years had been achieved by careful attention to detail, and by massaging all the usual ways of finding horsepower. The compression ratio, originally 8.5:1, had been raised to 9.7:1, the carburation had advanced from being a single downdraught Solex to twin dual-choke Weber 40DCO3 types (whose origins were in motor racing), while the porting, the exhaust system and every other detail had been carefully reworked.

The result was an urgent, high-revving little jewel of a power unit, which barked exuberantly about its business and always exhibited that characteristic 'gobble' noise from the carburettor intakes which the British came to know even better from the Lotus twin-cam power unit.

Matching it, and no less important in the scheme of things, was the 101-Series five-speed gearbox, the very first to be shown on an Alfa Romeo production car, the very first therefore to

be specified in a Giulietta, and vital to the way the car could go, or the way that it could be geared, overall, for road or track use. The five forward-gear layout had been achieved by adding a new and somewhat larger auxiliary casing to the rear of the main casing intended for the four-speed cluster, and squeezing in a fifth 'overdrive' pair of gears. The proof of this is found by comparing the internal ratios of the Giulietta four-speed and five-speed gearboxes:

Four-speed:　1.00, 1.357, 1.985, 3.258
Five-speed:　0.854, 1.00, 1.357, 1.985, 3.258

This method had been chosen instead of opting for the obvious late-1950s alternative, which was to specify a separate and rather bulky epicyclic overdrive, which was becoming increasingly popular on many British cars, including the fast-selling Triumph TR3. Although this was a novel and elegant technical solution at the time, such an engineering modification became familiar in many European cars in the next decade. If the five-speeder had been intended solely as a performance-improving feature, Alfa Romeo might have arranged for the final drive to be lowered, but in fact made no move to do this.

Although the Sprint Speciale became popular, if not legendary, in later years, it was a car that got off to an extremely slow start in the marketplace, as Alfa Romeo's own production figures demonstrate:

Year	Giulietta Sprint Speciales produced
1957	5
1958	11
1959	195
1960	200
1961	742
1962	213
Total	1,366

Until genuine series production began in 1959, the early cars were more specialized, still somewhat light and stripped out, and were often successful at club level in motor racing. At least 100 identically specified cars were needed to make this model eligible for use in sports car racing (some Alfa Romeo authorities suggest that rather less than this figure were actually built) and it took Bertone and Alfa Romeo up to 1959 to achieve this.

After that, it seems, Alfa Romeo and Bertone became reconciled to the fact that the little SZ Zagato had more sporty potential, and accordingly let the SS evolve into a normal road car. Justification of this policy came at once, for production rose sharply in 1959, reached a peak in 1961, before giving way to the 1.6-litre derivative in 1962, which sold just as well as the 1.3-litre type had ever done.

America's *Road & Track* magazine tested one of the steel-bodied Sprint Speciales in 1961, finding that it was, indeed, very different even from the Sprint Veloce which was owned by one of their staff writers:

Occasionally a car comes our way which is extra special. Unfortunately, the very interesting cars are usually very rare cars and we have to rely on friends to offer the family jewel for us to test . . . The bodywork, by Bertone, is flawless. The body construction is all steel with the exception of the aluminium deck lid, and every part of the Speciale that is visible is finished in excellent fashion. Doors, hood and trunk lid fit perfectly; the 'fair lines' across the panels match perfectly and the highlights indicate good panel forming. In short, it exudes quality.

Like the other Giuliettas, the Speciale leans considerably during hard cornering, but this goes almost unnoticed by the occupants of the car. Steering is neutral under most conditions but oversteer can be induced if the driver presses to the limit . . . The fact that the Giulietta is so vice-free has probably kept a good many mediocre drivers out of trouble, because it invites hard driving by its very nature

Overall impressions were good:

Taken as a road car, the Speciale is ideal: fast, comfortable, safe and economical insofar as gas mileage is

concerned. As a town car, it has some drawbacks: poor parking protection from any direction makes it almost impossible to park safely in either parallel parking or in the angle slots found in most market parking lots. The front overhang would also require that caution be used in angle parking near a curb of any height.

Road & Track's summary was very perceptive:

The Sprint Speciale is not a car that will appeal to every sports car enthusiast. The close to $6,000 [£2,143] price tag is pretty stiff when you consider that the main difference between the Speciale and the normal Sprint is the overdrive, a special body and the knowledge that you own a rare automobile from a highly regarded and reputable firm. In this latter statement we find the clue that helps justify the high cost.

By 1962, however, the SS was ready for revision, and this duly occurred in 1963, with a Giulia transplant. Alfa Romeo had in fact been planning this for some time, so when the new and larger Giulia saloon car was introduced, a new model called Giulia Sprint Speciale was already being prepared for launch.

Here was a typically resourceful piece of Alfa Romeo mix-and-match juggling. The new car's structure and styling were Giulietta Sprint Speciale, pure and simple, while (as with the Giulia 1600 Sprint described in Chapter 2) the engine/transmission/axle assemblies were all from the new Giulia model. The only way to identify the two cars was that the later (1.6-litre 'Giulia') versions carried the legend of 'Giulia SS' on the flanks, behind the front wheels and ahead of the passenger doors.

As with the 1600 Sprint, the engine was a highly tuned 112bhp at 6,500rpm power unit, more torquey than before, while the five-speed gearbox was shared in its entirety with the Giulia saloon and the 1600 Sprint. Not only that, but after the first 200 cars had been produced, this was the first SS-based Giulietta model to have front-wheel disc brakes, while there was a wholesale retouching of the interior.

Although the car's unladen weight had risen considerably – from 1,896lb (860kg) for the SS with the 1,290cc engine, to 2,095lb (950kg) for the Giulia Sprint Speciale with the 1,570cc type – so had the performance and the general flexibility. This was a car that would push the life of the SS body style successfully onwards until 1965, as follows:

Year	Giulia Sprint Speciales produced
1963	620
1964	676
1965	103
1966	1
Total :	1,400

In fact, more of these 1.6-litre-engined cars were sold than the original 1.3-litre cars that preceded them. The only problem was that no matter which country the cars were sold in, the Giulia SS was very costly. In Italy, for instance, the original Giulietta Sprint had been priced at 1,735,000 lira, the Giulietta Sprint Speciale came in at 2,400,000 lira, and in 1963 the Giulia Sprint Speciale cost 2,500,000 lira.

In the UK, therefore, in its road test of the Giulia Sprint Speciale, *Motor* magazine was justified in commenting that:

> In its own world, the Alfa Giulia Sprint Speciale is a fairly costly thoroughbred at nearly £2,400 from a firm with a racing ancestry which has now developed into a reputation for rather special road cars. For not much more than half the money there are three other cars which perform as well, and for a little less than the Alfa you can get one a third as fast again [this, of course, referred to Jaguar's extraordinary E-Type] – but none of these possesses any of the Alfa mystique nor even a distinction of rarity.

Motor, at least, found that this 112bhp-engined car could reach 113mph (181kph), and could sprint to 60mph (96kph) from rest in only 10.8 seconds, but that it could only pay for this with overall fuel consumption of 21mpg.

Even though it was quite overshadowed as a functional machine by the smaller SZ, the Sprint Speciale clearly appealed to a good many people, and over the years it must have been profitable for Bertone to build, and for Alfa Romeo to sell. One statistic alone – the sale of 2,766 cars – makes a telling point, as does the fact that this was the very last of the Giulietta-based family to remain on sale.

Zagato's Little Miracle

Zagato's own interpretation of the ultimate Giulietta was rather different from Bertone's. Where the Sprint Speciale was all about style, and all about development in a wind tunnel (or so it was claimed), Zagato simply settled down to make the smallest, lightest and most effective Giulietta of all time.

The result was the efficient and appealing little SZ (Sprint Zagato), which has always been one of my all-time favourite Alfa Romeos. Only ever produced as a two-seater coupé, with no compromises, it was as desirable as anything else on the market at the time.

Giulietta SZ Zagato (1957–62)

As for Giulietta Sprint Speciale, except for different, shorter, lighter body style:

Overall length	149.6in (3,800mm)
Overall width	61.0in (1,550mm)
Overall height	48.0in (1,220mm)
Unladen weight	1,698lb (770kg)–1,731lb (785kg), depending on specification.

First of all, let's look at the roots of the car – and of Zagato itself. Although this Milan-based coachbuilding/styling house had long-term links with Alfa Romeo, even by the end of the 1950s it had not forged profitable production contracts with them and was still concentrating on making its own lightweight concoctions, mainly for use in motorsport.

Zagato

Ugo Zagato, originally a metal worker in Cologne, then in an Italian aircraft factory, set up his own small coachbuilding business in Milan in 1919. Serried ranks of gorgeous Spider and coupé styles on 1920s and 1930s racing Alfa Romeos made the Zagato name famous, but after Allied bombers destroyed his factory in 1943, he struggled to start again after the war.

By that time Ugo's son Elio had joined the firm, and the company continued to expand. Like others – Bertone and Pininfarina, for instance – growth came from taking on limited-run contracts for larger concerns who would not tackle such projects themselves.

The first small-engined Alfa to get the Bertone treatment was the cute and formidably successful Giulietta SZ coupé of the late 1950s. The noisy but extremely fast Giulia TZ followed it, but the first true Zagato-bodied Alfa road car was the pretty little GT 1300 Junior Z coupé of 1969.

Zagato went further upmarket in the 1970s and 1980s, working for Aston Martin and Maserati, but there was still time to produce the startling SZ of 1989. As with most of its previous forms, the SZ caused a great deal of discussion – it would not have been a Zagato style without that!

The Alfa/motorsport connection had been forged way back in the 1920s. Some of the most elegant 6C 1500 and 6C 1750 sports cars, including major motor racing victors, had been bodied by Zagato, as had many strikingly shaped supercharged 8C 2300s of the 1930s. More recently, though, Zagato had spent time working with Lancia, and Alfa had come to favour Touring, Bertone and Pininfarina.

The Giulietta SZ project, therefore, started as a private Zagato venture (Elio Zagato wanted a car in which he could compete for himself), and it was only after hand-built cars had proved themselves in motorsport that Alfa Romeo officially welcomed it into the family, and saw to it that Zagato would build the monocoque-cum-tubular-frame-supported shells in reasonable quantities – indeed, large quantities by existing Zagato standards.

Zagato's private-venture cars evolved through an association with the Conrero tuning shop, and individually-built cars whose styling gradually edged towards that of the SZ 'production' car were successful long before they became official models.

As with Bertone's Sprint Speciale, this was a project that started in 1957, when Alfa Romeo let it be known that they could supply platforms and rolling chassis fitted with the very latest 100bhp/1,290cc engine and the brand-new 101-style five-speed gearbox. Zagato, like Bertone,

was electrified by this news, and made haste to add its own special flavour to such a chassis.

What happened in the next three years – between Zagato starting work, and Alfa Romeo officially launching the SZ at the Geneva Motor Show of March 1960 – is rather hazy. According to Alfa Romeo's own records, only a single SZ was built in 1957, but none was produced in 1958 and 1959, after which the first sixty-one 'production cars' were assembled in 1960.

Even so, early examples of cars which evolved into the SZ shape certainly appeared in motorsport in 1958 – one privately-owned, French-registered car not only won the French Alpine rally outright in July 1958, but six weeks later went on to win the gruelling Liège-Rome-Liège marathon – and there were increasingly high-profile appearances on the race tracks.

What must be assumed – and where Italian history is concerned, that is always a difficult thing to do – is that early cars, built in penny numbers, were produced privately by Zagato, with little overt Alfa Romeo connection; it was only from early 1960 that the link became official.

Although the original SZs looked very similar to the cars that went on sale in 1960, there were certainly styling, if not technical differences. Having looked carefully at the coupé body shells that Zagato made for the Lancia Appia GTE chassis from 1957, I can also see distinct family likenesses, and as far as the early Giulietta SZs were concerned, I suspect that there were some common panels and detailing under the two skins.

Even so, the base of the SZ was never in doubt. Like the Sprint Speciale, it was built up on the short-wheelbase (88.6in (2,250mm)) version of the successful Giulietta platform – that normally found under the Pininfarina-made Spider model.

That the SZ is not a well-known car does not excuse one other Alfa author for crediting it with a 'spaceframe chassis', which it most assuredly did not have. The platform, of course, was pressed-steel, as was some of the inner and structural bodywork, though a framework of body tubing supporting a number of external panels were in thin-gauge aluminium. Original cars had perspex side and rear windows, though in later life a number had these replaced with glass. Discreet 'Z' badges on the front wings told those who knew

about these things that it was Zagato who had conceived it.

Also like the Sprint Speciale, it accommodated the highly tuned 100bhp/1,290cc twin-cam engine, was backed by the brand new five-speed 'overdrive' gearbox, and used the same 4.555:1 rear axle ratio. Plus, of course, it had a large fuel tank, which made it ideal for use in longer distance sports car races.

Hidden away, therefore, was the same mechanical package that featured in the Sprint Speciale, but it was in the bodywork that the Zagato-styled car was so different. From every angle, and from every philosophical viewpoint, this was a completely different type of car from the Sprint Speciale.

Rounded rather than consciously styled, compact rather than flamboyant, and with so little decoration that without the famous Alfa Romeo shield grille up front it might have been difficult

This is one of my favourite Alfas – the Zagato-styled Giulietta SZ (or Sprint Zagato). Shorter, lighter and stubbier than the normal Sprint, this was a competition car, pure and in the raw, which shared its running gear with the Sprint Speciale.

Not only did the Giulietta SZ look exactly right for its purpose – circuit racing and rallying – but it was much lighter and much more powerful than the series-production Sprint. Only 200 of these excellent little projectiles were ever built.

to recognize, here was a stubby little car whose purpose was to cover up the running gear and occupants, and to slip through the air as easily as possible, all at the lowest possible weight.

To quote *Autocar's* Geneva Show report of 1960:

> Although the wheelbase and track are also identical [to the Sprint Speciale], the car is lower and shorter and – of more importance in relation to performance – lighter. With a dry weight of 14.8cwt [1,658lb (752kg)], the claimed maximum speed of 130mph appears possible. As might be expected from a company with such a background of sporting products, the driving position, and particularly the support given by the amply ventilated seats, would be difficult to improve.

Compared with the Sprint Speciale, the major dimensional differences in the SZ were in the length and the width. Not only was the Zagato-bodied car a full 4.6in (11.7cm) narrower than the Bertone, but it was also 17.3in (439mm) shorter, this being a very large gain indeed, made almost entirely at the expense of front and rear overhang dimensions.

Although the SZ's shape was simple in the extreme, this was an attractive package, subtly rounded in a nature-perfect ovoidal sort of way. With virtually no rear overhang at all, with a thoroughly rounded nose, and with perspex side windows which sloped in heavily towards the roof, this style spelt 'purpose' rather than 'elegance', and looked all the better for it.

There was very little luggage accommodation, but who carried luggage in a motor race? Neither were there plush seats, thick carpets, glossy trim or bumpers. The result was an Alfa as agile

An interesting SZ study, on a motor show stand in Europe, where the overhead lighting shows off the lines rather effectively. This is one of the last cars, with the extended nose and tail and relocated side lamps – really a precursor of the Giulia TZ which would follow.

There may be no decoration and a stark interior, but compared with the Sprint, the important features of the SZ were that it had 100bhp (instead of 90bhp), five speeds (instead of four), and weighed only 1,698lb (770kg) (instead of the Sprint Veloce's 1,973lb (895kg)). Its power-weight ratio was therefore 30 per cent better and there was a better transmission, too!

Although the body style of the late-1950s Sprint Speciale was unique, the facia was almost the same as that used in the Giulietta Sprint. Amazing, though, that there was an 'umbrella handle' handbrake on such a car!

An early example of the Zagato-bodied Giulietta SZ, which won the incredibly rough and tough Liège-Rome-Liège rally of 1958 (driven by Bernard Consten and Jean Hebert), but all is not what it seems ...

The rear end style of the early Zagato-bodied Giulietta SZ, which also won the French Alpine rally, is a different shape from that which 'officially' went on sale in 1960.

on its wheels as a cat on its paws, a car dedicated to speed, in a straight line or around corners, a car in which comfort did not appear to have been a consideration, for the seats were hard, unforgiving, non-adjustable, and must have been purgatory on long journeys.

But it was fast, forgiving, accelerative and – above all – light. In 1960 Alfa Romeo's officially quoted figure for the unladen weight was 1,731lb (785kg), and you may be sure that Zagato's earliest cars, and those prepared for out-and-out top-quality motorsport, were lighter still.

This was the sort of Giulietta that Alfa customers needed for their sport – 242lb (110kg) lighter even than the Giulietta Sprint Veloce, more powerful and (because of the short wheelbase and race-tuned handling) considerably more manoeuvrable than any other Giulietta. Yet the racing, and particularly the rallying successes notched up by these cars, confirm that the vital underpinnings – platform, running gear and suspension – were all solidly engineered, making the SZ an ideal purchase for private owners.

As other authorities have pointed out, it is the Italian coachbuilder's way of things that no two SZs were ever necessarily alike – some having exposed headlamps, some with perspex covers, some with perspex windows, and some with glass windows – but all were phenomenally quick little machines.

It's easy to look back more than forty years and consider a measured top speed of about 120mph (193kph) rather ordinary, but by 1960 standards it was phenomenal. Those were still the days when the only road cars to go faster than 130mph (209kph) were Ferraris and Maseratis, along with the Mercedes-Benz 300SL, and these were the Supercars of the era. The SZ was no Supercar, but it was undoubtedly super-efficient.

North America's *Road & Track* magazine, which tested an Italian-based SZ in 1961, certainly thought so. Noting the large proportion of aluminium in the bodywork, and the fact that the seats were only lightly padded, they must have faced up to a 2,000-mile road trip with some trepidation. Even so:

> These [seats] hold the occupants firmly and with reasonable comfort, but for long distances, a little more padding – particularly along the lateral struts – and a more solid base cushion would be desirable . . . This car, of course, is intended to be driven with the straight-arm technique. Even so, the range of lengthwise seat adjustment is exceptional. Others please follow – you too, E-Type!

Amazingly, the official road cars (as opposed to race cars, which underwent further lightening and stripping out) were fitted with a full heating-defrosting system, as was available in the Sprint Speciale, but sun visors were not provided.

Naturally the testers found the handling to be well up to the straight-line performance (0–100mph in 33.4 seconds, and no less than 107mph (172kph) in fourth gear):

> We said that the car always goes faster than it feels: this can be attributed to the free-revving engine, the unmistakably sure-footed chassis and a really low level of wind noise. Added to this is the knowledge of having [drum] brakes able to cope with any situation – even repeated high-speed braking during performance tests failed to produce fade.

Good, very good indeed, but not perfect, as Alfa Romeo and Zagato were already finding out. Despite the glowing reports from customers and testers, there is no doubt that the SZ was not as aerodynamically sound as hoped. Accordingly, for 1961–62, and for the building of the final batch of 30 SZs, a revised version was put on sale. Longer than before because of an extended nose and tail profile, with different side and tail window shapes, with faired-in headlamps and with a sharply cut-off 'Kamm' tail, this 'SZ2' (as some people called it) was not only a lineal descendant of the original SZ, but also a direct ancestor of the Giulia-based Tubolare Zagato (TZ) (*see* Chapter 5).

The running gear of the 'SZ2' was little changed, though the fitment of front-wheel disc brakes instead of the original three-shoe drums was a distinct advance. Amazingly, Alfa Romeo claimed that it was slightly lighter than before – by 33lb (15kg).

The SZ, though, was a limited-market model, with a limited life, and this is Alfa Romeo's own summary of numbers built:

Year	Sprint Zagatos produced
1957	1
1958	–
1959	–
1960	61
1961	112
1962	36
Total	210

Unlike the Sprint Speciale, however, the SZ was never given a final upgrade by the fitting of the Giulia engine. Zagato was more ambitious, and Alfa Romeo was more inclined to indulge them at this point, so the result was the arrival of the Zagato-built Giulia-based Tubolare Zagato in 1963.

Motorsport Successes

Although the Sprint Speciale was faster than every mainstream Giulietta, its record on the track was invariably overshadowed by the exploits of the little Zagato-inspired SZ. Alfa Romeo historian David Owen once wrote that the SS was 'almost too pretty to race' which, to many minds, it most certainly was.

Even in 1957, the prototype Zagato-built 'specials' started winning their class in Italian hill climbs, but it was in 1958 that the resourceful pairing of Bernard Consten and Roger de Laganeste took outright victory in the French Alpine rally. Amazingly enough, only weeks later the same French-registered car then won the rough, tough, fast, loose, dusty and utterly exhausting Liège-Rome-Liège marathon, Consten being partnered by Hebert on this occasion.

I must stress the importance of these victories over those on the circuits, simply because condi-

tions were so much more demanding and the cars' chassis had to work so much harder. The fact that the car completed one fast rally (the Alpine) and followed it up with triumph in the Liège-Rome-Liège, which was always recognized as a real 'breakers' yard', was truly astonishing.

That this was no fluke was proved two years later when, in June 1960, another French-registered SZ won the French Alpine rally, this driven by Roger de Laganeste and Henri Greder. And this wasn't achieved by using a favourable handicap, for it came in a tough event where only six cars competed the course without losing any time on the road, and where every other car had a much larger engine.

The SZ's racing successes, naturally enough, were mainly confined to class and category victories, though the little Alfas were always respected, if not feared, in all locations. Over the years there would be successes at Monza, Sebring (Florida, USA), Pescara (Italy), Daytona (USA) and in the Targa Florio in Italy. And even though twenty-four flat-out hours was really too much for this highly tuned little engine, one car finished in a creditable tenth place at Le Mans in 1962, averaging 97.73mph (157kph), and achieving a timed top speed of no less than 135mph (217kph).

And there would be more of this sort of outstanding performance in the years to come.

Giulietta Coupé Family – Production Figures

1,290cc engine

Sprint	24,084
Sprint Veloce	3,058
Sprint Speciale (Bertone)	1,366
SZ (Zagato)	200
1300 Sprint	1,900

1,570cc engine

Sprint	7,107
Sprint Speciale (Bertone)	1,400
Total :	39,115

Alfa Romeo Giulietta Performance

This is a summary of the figures achieved by the world's most authoritative magazines, *Autocar* and *Road and Track*, of cars supplied for test over the years:

Model	Giulietta Sprint	Giulietta Sprint Speciale (Bertone)	Giulietta Sprint SZ (Zagato)	Giulia Sprint (Giulietta style)	Giulia Sprint Speciale (Bertone style)
	1,290cc 80bhp	1,290cc 100bhp	1,290cc 100bhp	1,570cc 92bhp	1,570cc 112bhp
Max. speed					
(mph)	103	120	120	108	113
Acceleration (sec)					
0–60mph	13.2	12.3	11.2	13.2	10.8
0–80mph	25.8	21.8	19.1	24.7	20.1
0–100mph	–	38.0	33.4	53.8	33.5
Standing $\frac{1}{4}$–mile (sec)	19.2	18.4	17.8	18.8	18.0
Consumption (mpg)					
Overall	-	–	–	26.7	21.0
Typical	-	–	–	30	26
Kerb weight (lb (kg))	2,090 (948)	2,110 (957)	2,220 (1,007)	2,142 (972)	2,195 (995)
Year tested	1961	1961	1961	1963	1965
Tested by	*Road and Track*	*Road and Track*	*Road and Track*	*Autocar*	*Autocar*

4 Giulia Sprint – The Mainstream Cars

Picture an Alfa Romeo board meeting in the late 1950s: the Giulietta range was selling well, the new, large 2000 was holding its own, and great ambitions were in the air. The company was thinking about its future – but what future?

Alfa Romeo, it was thought, should plan to make more cars, and to sell more cars overseas. Although it could not compete with Fiat at home, it could certainly square up to Lancia. And, although it had to charge more money for the privilege, it was already able to match what MG and Triumph were doing in the USA.

By 1959 the Giulietta family was already five years old and, technically at least, it was at its peak, though sales were continuing to rise. The directors hoped that more than 30,000 cars would be built in 1960 (in fact the output would be 33,606 Giuliettas and 3,009 2000s). Which meant that the Portello factory, the ageing mono-lith which had been painstakingly re-created in

Having outgrown its Portello factory, in the early 1960s Alfa Romeo developed the new Arese factory just outside the city.

the 1950s, was now bursting at the seams.

So it was decision day. Not only would Alfa Romeo evolve a new family of cars, they would also build a brand new factory. The result was the arrival of the new Giulia saloon car range in 1962, and the Arese factory in which to assemble them.

New Thinking

We all know that the Giulia platform, engine and running gear were logical evolutions of the exist-ing Giulietta, but not everyone knows that this was not the first car considered by the directors to flesh out the range. That car was in fact the front-wheel-drive 'Tipo 103'.

In 1959–60, Alfa's decision was not to replace the Giulietta directly, but to add another model to the line-up. One way or another, they were looking for increased volume. The options, as they saw them, were to produce a larger car than the Giulietta, or a smaller car to slot into the range under it. Smaller cars usually meant cheaper cars, and cheaper cars meant increased sales, which would deliver greatly increased volumes.

Initially, therefore, Tipo 103 took shape as a car smaller than the Giulietta saloon (it was only 143in (3,630mm) long), and was given front-wheel-drive with a transversely mounted 896cc twin-cam engine and a new four-speed gear-box/transaxle. The styling of the only prototype constructed was that of a boxy four-door saloon.

This new car worked, and worked well, but was side-lined when the implications of new transmission tooling and all-new suspension and body-shell tooling costs were realized. Shelved almost at once, the prototype was put into stor-age, and will reappear briefly in Chapter 7. (At this time Alfa Romeo was assembling Renault Dauphines under licence in Italy, but it is proba-bly a red herring to suggest that the Tipo 103's styling influenced the shape of the Renault R8 which followed.)

The alternative, therefore, was to approve the design of a range of cars, the Tipo 105s, to be called Giulia, which would be bigger than the Giulietta in all respects – with a bigger platform, bigger engines, a bigger range of derivatives, and selling at a higher price. In marketing terms, there would be a slight overlap with the Giulietta, but this was not expected to last indefinitely. At the same time, the existing range of large 2000 mod-els would be upgraded with a six-cylinder 2.6-litre engine.

All this was a classic product planning solution to broaden Alfa Romeo's showroom appeal. From 1962, when the new Giulia made its debut, there would be 1.3-litre Giuliettas from 62bhp to 74bhp, projected Giulias with 92bhp and (in

---

Arese – a New Factory

With the old Portello plant incapable of further expansion by the late 1950s, Alfa Romeo had to build a new factory in the 1960s, and eventually settled on undeveloped land at Arese. Up to that point, this had been a peaceful little village just a few miles north of the centre of Milan, but conveniently close to the autostrada network.

The Arese site had many advantages – it was large, it was on flat land, it was still close to Milan and its tra-ditional workforce, and it was available. Since Alfa Romeo was controlled by the IRI, a government-financed organization, no planning permission prob-lems were ever anticipated – or appeared.

Here it was that Alfa Romeo constructed a massive new plant, with a theoretical capacity of 150,000 vehi-cles every year (four times the numbers being built when planning began in 1959–60). As well as the pro-duction lines, the administrative office blocks, design and technical centre, and the archive/museum build-ings were centred there.

The new Giulia range, when launched in 1962, started its career in the old Portello factory, but it was not long before the Arese plant came on stream in 1963. Alfa Romeo claimed, proudly, that the Giulia Sprint GT was the first model to be built entirely at Arese. After this, all other Giulia family members, and later Alfettas and their descendants, were assembled there, though engine and other mechanical parts con-tinued to be machined at Portello, though not the flat-four-engined front-wheel-drive Alfasuds or the 33s which took over from them. These were specially designed to be produced at another new factory, close to Naples, in the south of Italy.

Arese is the centre of all Alfa Romeo activity to this day.

prospect) 98bhp, and the 2600 with 130bhp. Not only that, but Alfa also planned, eventually, to market saloons, coupés, Spiders and even (in the Giulia's case) estate cars. No wonder the company needed a new factory, at Arese, to accept them all.

Alfa Romeo had learned a lot from the launch, the development, the evolution and the still-evolving career of the Giuliettas, and was once again determined to carve every possible derivative out of the same basic design. The saloon version (Giulia TI) would appear first, the new engine would be applied to sporting Giuliettas (Sprint, Spider and SS) at once, a Bertone-manufactured coupé style would follow within a year (the Sprint GT), and there would then be a new Spider, planned for the mid-1960s.

Alfa Romeo revealed the new-generation Giulia in 1962. Built on a new platform, it used the same basic drive line as the Giulietta, but this time with a 1,570cc version of the engine and a five-speed gearbox. This was the 98bhp Super model of 1965.

The Giulia TI, introduced in this boxy guise in 1962, had a 92bhp/1.6-litre version of the famous twin-cam engine, but very undistinguished styling.

Then the fun – and the complications – would really begin. Before long there would be smaller-engined saloons and high-power/lightweight saloons, a convertible version of the coupé, a high-power/lightweight coupé, a tubular-framed 'homologation special' (the TZ), and more.

New Platform

As with the Giulietta, this could only be done if the 'chassis' platform was arranged to accept a variety of body styles and more than one wheelbase. Alfa Romeo already knew about such

Bertone, given the task of shaping a new coupé around the platform of the undistinguished Giulia saloon, produced this ultra-smart GT in 1963. Recognition points included the big round headlamps and the simple mesh grille.

things, and were quite prepared to repeat the successful Giulietta strategy.

Although much of the new car's running gear looked familiar to Alfa-watchers, there were changes in all departments. In particular, the basis of these cars would be a brand new platform and underbody – one which Alfa Romeo was ready to commit to a decade of life. In the end, the platform's life was an astonishing thirty-one years, as the last of the much-changed Spiders was not produced until 1993.

That the platform was new, and not merely a stretch of the Giulietta's underpan, is confirmed by a look at the new car's front suspension layouts, the rear suspension location, and by some basic dimensions. In particular, the positioning of the main mounting points for the double-wishbone front suspension, and the massive architecture of the new 'A-bracket' at the rear, made a new underbody superstructure absolutely essential.

The following dimensions show how the first of the Giulia saloons stacked up against the early 1960s Giulietta:

Feature	Giulia	Giulietta	Increase
Wheelbase	98.8in (2,509mm)	93.7in (2,380mm)	5.1in (129mm)
Overall length	165.6in (4,206mm)	157.0in (3,990mm)	8.6in (216mm)
Front track	51.6in (1,310mm)	50.9in (1,290mm)	0.7in (20mm)
Rear track	50.0in (1,270mm)	50.0in (1,270mm)	No increase

Before considering the technicalities of this new-generation car, the style of the Giulia TI saloon (the first of the new family to be put on sale) should be analysed. Not because it was anonymous, but because it was so unexpected.

The Giulietta had been such a neat, understated, but nevertheless attractive four-door style, and I am sure that every Alfa-watcher was expecting to see an even more refined shape on the new car. Not so. It was certainly a four-door saloon shape, which imposed all manner of compromises on the designers, but the new car was undeniably craggy.

Alfa Romeo, however, was totally proud of what it had produced (there had been no input from outside styling houses; or if there was, no credit was ever given) for the interior was considerably more spacious than before, and they claimed a very creditable drag coefficient of just 0.34. The public never seemed to have any doubts, for in the 1960s, this became the best-selling Alfa Romeo of all.

It was, at least, immediately recognizable, for it had a short bonnet/front-end, four headlamps in a bluff nose, a large and panoramic windscreen, a wrap-round rear glass and a sharply squared-off tail: naturally, the famous Alfa. Yet although the Giulia saloon looked larger than the Giulietta had been, it was almost exactly the same width and the same unladen height as before.

Technically, though, the interesting elements were all hidden away, in the running gear and the suspension. First of all, the engine, transmission and rear axle were all direct, linear and recognizable developments of Giulietta components, which meant that Alfa Romeo was getting everything it could out of its original tooling investment. As before, the much-loved little twin-cam engine was installed at a slight angle in the engine bay – leaning perceptibly towards the left (exhaust) side – and retained a single, downdraught carburettor, but had been enlarged from 1,290cc to 1,570cc, as demonstrated below:

Feature	Giulia	Giulietta
Capacity (cc)	1,570	1,290
Bore (mm)	78	74
Stroke (mm)	82	75

At first, this looks as if nothing more complicated had been needed than a longer-stroke crankshaft and wider-bore 'wet' liners, but structurally more serious changes had been made. Although the extra stroke – all of 0.275in (7mm), half of which would have been needed above the line of the crankshaft – might have been accommodated within the confines of the original cylinder block, Alfa Romeo chose to deepen the cylinder-block casting by an appropriate amount.

This was done for several reasons, including the detail design of the pistons, and the fact that even at this stage Alfa Romeo was thinking further ahead to yet greater enlargement of the engine in future years and for yet-to-be-designed models. One obvious visual difference, incidentally, was that the mechanical petrol pump of the 1,290cc engine, originally fixed to the front of the aluminium cylinder head, was no longer there.

No matter. Here was an engine which was not only much torquier than before, but one which was still capable of revving high and sweetly. All the technically desirable cylinder-head elements – part-spherical combustion chambers, twin-overhead camshaft operation of the valves, and well-shaped inlet and exhaust valves – were still present, and we already knew just how successful the smaller-engined types had been in motorsport. It was not long before further motorsport success followed for the 1.6-litre-engined type.

Backing this engine was the latest version of the Giulietta/101-style five-speed gearbox. However, although this was still a classic 'overdrive' five-speeder, the intermediate internal gearbox ratios were all marginally different, this being due to a rearrangement of the number of teeth in the box itself.

If five speeds had become standard on the saloon, it was assumed that a five-speeder must surely figure in the sporting types when they eventually appeared, and so it proved.

Except for some subtle updating and strengthening, the structure and design of the hypoid-bevel beam rear axle of the new car was exactly like that of the Giulietta (which continued, of course). The cast centre casing was in aluminium, the tubes were in steel, and the long-established wheel track of 50.0in (1,270mm) had been retained. Because this was a heavier car, however,

the ratio was 5.125:1, which compared with 4.555:1 for the Giulietta.

Although the independent front suspension was still by coil springs, double wishbones, telescopic dampers and a stout anti-roll torsion bar, the detail construction and, I suspect, the geometry were different from that of the Giulietta. In particular, the vertical link (king post) of the Giulia was much shorter than before, the telescopic dampers and the springs were now separated (they had been mounted concentrically in the Giulietta), the coils being vertically aligned and fatter than before, while the dampers were positioned behind the line of the bottom wishbones.

At first glance, the rear suspension of the Giulia looked so substantial as to have been designed for a much heavier car, but in detail it was only a little heavier than before. The object, it seems, had been to control axle movements even more precisely – and this had certainly been achieved.

As with the front end, however, although the basic intent might have been the same as for the Giulietta, the hardware was different. As before, suspension was by coil springs, and axle location was by twin trailing arms and an above-axle A-bracket (or a T-piece), but detail execution was new. Coil spring/damper units, which had been above the line of the axle, were now ahead of it in the Giulia installation, and bore down on the trailing arms themselves, the Giulia being a car that also had larger and carefully shaped rubber bump-stop snubbers above the axle tubes.

The trailing arms carried a much more substantial cross-section (in the Giulietta they had been tubular, but now they were channel-section pressings), but it was the upper A-bracket/T-piece which caused great interest. That of the Giulietta had been conventional, truly 'A'-shaped and tubular, but on the Giulia was a much more solid device, a combined tubular and pressings assembly, with widely spaced chassis mountings ahead of the line of the coil spring/damper units, and tying up to the familiar axle casing mounting lug above the crown wheel itself.

The braking system also caused much comment for, quite ahead of the trends that had spread all around Europe, on the initial Giulia saloon car (but never the sporty types) they were drums and not discs. Front drums, indeed, featured three leading shoes, rather like those fairly recently blooded on the competition Sprint Speciale and SZ types.

Here, I suspect, was an element of stubbornness from Alfa Romeo. Anxious to spend no more money than absolutely necessary (and this was still a period when disc brake technology was relatively expensive to replicate), Alfa Romeo insisted that the three-shoe drum brake installation was still right for the job.

In which case, why did Alfa Romeo then change their minds so speedily, so that well before the Sprint GT Coupé was launched in September 1963, the Giulia chassis had been converted to four-wheel Dunlop disc brakes? In fact, only 22,000 Giulia models – all of them TI saloons – were ever manufactured with drum brakes. Each and every Giulia Sprint GT would have disc brakes.

Sprint GT – Giugiaro's Genius

Right from the start of the Tipo 105/Giulia project, Bertone of Turin had been consulted regularly about the evolution of a new coupé body style. Bertone's stylists would shape the new car, but full-scale production would take place at the new Arese factory. Both companies had every reason to be happy about this.

The Giulia Sprint GT of 1963 was another classic Bertone style. It was the first of a long-running series of these machines.

In 1963 the new Giulia Sprint GT ran on a shorter wheelbase version of the saloon's platform, and the compact cabin style meant that it was, at best, a 2+2 seater. Flawless, even so.

For Giulietta lovers, the engine of the Giulia Sprint GT looked familiar enough, but this time it had 1,570cc, twin horizontal Weber carburettors, and 106bhp. It was neat, though, and there was enough space for servicing when the time came.

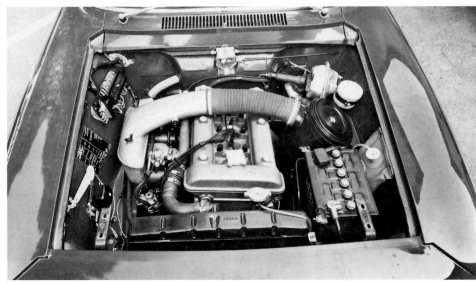

Alfa Romeo, on the one hand, was delighted with the long-running success of the original Bertone-styled Giulietta Sprints, while Bertone was pleased to have used this – and other – Alfa Romeo contracts to build up its business. Faced with the exciting prospect of producing hundreds of extra shells every week, Bertone was already looking forward to erecting a new factory in Grugliasco, a suburb of Turin.

To shape a new Giulia-based coupé in the early 1960s, Bertone had a secret weapon: the amazingly talented Giorgetto Giugiaro, who had joined the company from the Fiat styling studio in 1959. The story goes that Giugiaro had been called up to do his Italian military National Service in 1960, that the Bertone company pulled any number of strings, made sure that he was not kept too busy, and had him style the new Giulia Sprint GT, a task which he accomplished in March and April 1960. Giugiaro then turned his attention to the smaller Alfa Romeo, and used many of the same styling cues to get a result.

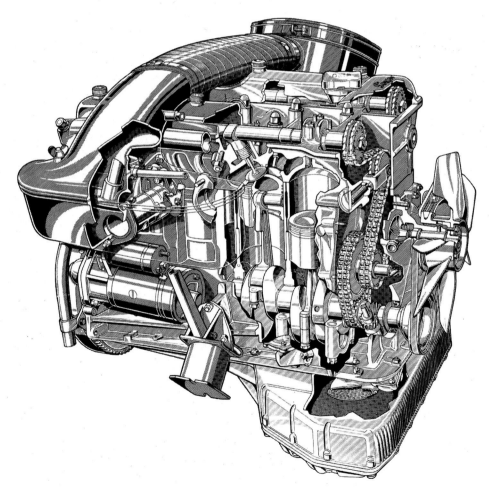

Students of engineering who studied this cutaway drawing of the Giulia Sprint GT engine reckoned that the limits of bore size had already been approached. They were right. In 1.6-litre form it had a 78mm bore; even the full 2-litre engine only had an 84mm bore.

Giulia Sprint GT/GTV (1963–77, all types)

Layout

Unit-construction body-chassis structure, with steel panels. Two-door, front engine/rear drive, sold as 2+2-seater coupé model.

Engine

Block material	Cast aluminium
Head material	Cast aluminium
Cylinders	4 in-line
Cooling	Water
Main bearings	5
Valves	2 per cylinder, operated by twin-overhead camshafts and inverted bucket-type tappets, driven by chain from crankshaft

GT 1300 Junior, 1,290cc: bore and stroke 74 × 75mm; compression ratio 8.5:1; two horizontal twin-choke Weber 40DCOE28 carburettors; 89bhp (DIN) @ 6,000rpm, 101lb ft @ 3,200rpm

GT, 1,570cc: bore and stroke 78 × 82mm; compression ratio 9.0:1; two horizontal twin-choke Weber 40DCOE 4 carburettors; 106bhp (DIN) @ 6,000rpm, 103lb ft @ 3,000rpm

GT Veloce, 1,570cc: bore and stroke 78 × 82mm; compression ratio 9.0:1; two horizontal twin-choke Weber 40DCOE27 carburettors; 109bhp (DIN) @ 6,000rpm, 105lb ft @ 2,800rpm

1750 GT Veloce, 1,779cc: bore and stroke 80 × 88.5mm; compression ratio 9.5:1; two horizontal twin-choke Weber 40DCOE 32 carburettors; 122bhp (DIN) @ 5,500rpm, 127lb ft @ 2,900rpm
(Note: SPICA fuel-injection on USA-market cars)

2000 GTV, 1,962cc: bore and stroke 84 × 88.5mm; compression ratio 9.0:1; two horizontal twin-choke Weber 40DCOE carburettors, Solex C40 DDH-5 or Dellorto DHLA40 types; 132bhp (DIN) @ 5,500rpm, 134lb ft @ 3,000rpm
(Note: SPICA fuel-injection on USA-market cars)

Transmission

Five-speed all-synchromesh manual gearbox

Clutch	Single dry plate; hydraulically operated

Internal Gearbox Ratios

Top	0.791
4th	1.00
3rd	1.355
2nd	1.988
1st	3.304
Reverse	3.010
Final drive	4.555:1, except 4.1:1 on 2000 GT Veloce

Suspension and Steering

Front	Independent, coil springs, wishbones, anti-roll bar, telescopic dampers

Giulia Sprint GT/GTV (1963–77, all types) *continued*	
Rear	Live (beam) axle, by coil springs, radius arms, A-bracket, telescopic dampers. Anti-roll bar on 1750/2000 types
Steering	Recirculating ball, or worm and roller
Tyres	155-15 radial-ply on 1.3/1.6-litre models
	165-14in on 1750/2000 models
Wheels	Steel disc, bolt-on
Rim width	4.5in on 1.3/1.6-litre models, 5.5in on 1750/2000 models
Brakes	
Type	Disc brakes at front and rear, hydraulically operated
Size	11.25in front discs, 9.75in dia. rear discs
	(10.5in dia. rear discs, 1965)
Dimensions	
Track	
Front	51.5in (1,310mm)
Rear	50.1in (1,270mm)
Wheelbase	92.5in (2,350mm)
Overall length	160.5in (4,080mm)
Overall width	62.2in (1,580mm)
Overall height	51.7in (1,315mm)
Unladen weight	2,090lb (948kg)–2,292lb (1,040kg)

Alfa Romeo, in the meantime, had changed its policy a little. Whereas Bertone had been obliged to shape the Giulietta Sprint around the unchanged wheelbase/platform of the then-secret Giulietta saloon, the new car was to be supplied with a shortened version of the new Giulia platform. However, not many people realize that even this shortened wheelbase was longer than that of the original Giulietta.

For the Bertone-styled Giulia Sprint GT, the wheelbase was shortened by 6.3in (160mm) – from 98.8in (2,510mm) to 92.5in (2,350mm) – but this was not the end of the story. Alfa Romeo was preparing to produce three different wheelbase derivatives, for the platform to be used on the forthcoming Pininfarina-styled Spider/Duetto would be even shorter.

Like any accomplished artist, at this time Giugiaro was developing and evolving his visual themes on several fronts, so it is not surprising that the style of the new Alfa should look very much like that of the Alfa 2000/2600 Sprint, and

that it was even possible to see some 'cues' repeated in the Gordon-Keeble of the same period.

Because the Giulia Sprint GT was intended to have a more roomy cabin – it was meant to be a regular 2+2 (later, as we shall see, Alfa Romeo even managed to convince the motorsport authorities that it was a four-seater!) – the shell was somewhat bulkier than that of the Giulietta Sprint.

The table opposite shows how the sporting Giulia had not only put on bulk, but weight, too.

Clearly Giugiaro had not only developed a sure eye for a line, or for a proportion, but while he was at Fiat he had also learned a lot about packaging. Even though the Giulia Sprint GT's cabin was based on a slightly shorter wheelbase than that of the Giulietta Sprint, by using a subtly more squared-up profile with a more vertical rear window it allowed considerably more passenger space in the rear seat.

When the public first saw the car, at the Frankfurt Motor Show of September 1963, they found

Comparison: Giulia Sprint GT and Giulietta Sprint

Feature	Giulia Sprint GT	Giulietta Sprint Veloce	Difference
Wheelbase	92.5in (2,350mm)	93.7in (2,380mm)	1.2in (30mm) shorter
Overall length	160.5in (4,080mm)	156.5in (3,975mm)	4.0in (105mm) increase
Width	62.2in (1,580mm)	60.5in (1,537mm)	1.7in (43mm) increase
Height (unladen)	51.7in (1,315mm)	52.0in (1,321mm)	0.3in (6mm) decrease
Weight (unladen)	2,090lb (948kg)	1,973lb (895kg)	117lb (53kg) increase

the style totally distinctive. One fascinating detail was the slight step in the shroud presswork around the front of the bonnet, and the way that the front of the bonnet itself was slightly, but definitely, proud of that shroud.

The facia/instrumentation layout of the new car was at once more pleasing and advanced than that of the Giulietta had ever been, yet was rather tacky in its detailing. It was all very well providing a neat instrument layout, but did the dials have to be inserted into a Fablon-covered dashboard? Was a rather basic two-spoke steering wheel justifed, and was it really acceptable to offer only moulded rubber mats on the floor instead of proper carpets? At least the gearchange was central, and standard (though a steering column change was still to be found in the saloon-car derivatives).

Mechanically, and compared with the new Giulia TI saloon, the major improvement was to the engine. By Alfa Romeo twin-cam standards, whereas the saloon's engine and its single down-draught carburettor looked distinctly ordinary, that fitted to the Sprint GT looked sporty, purposeful, and definitely more powerful.

As on the Giulietta Sprint Veloce, and the special-modified Giuliettas, here was an engine that looked as if it meant business – and it did! The twin-cam head was matched to two twin-choke horizontal Weber carburettors which, when allied to sporty camshaft profiles and a 9.0:1 compression ratio, liberated 106bhp (DIN) at 6,000rpm. Although this was still not as much as had already been put on sale in the latest Giulia TI Super Saloon and the TZ models, both of these cars, of course, being intended for competition use, it was a good start for what would presumably be a long career and several other derivatives. And it was enough to give the new Giulia Sprint GT a top speed of at least 110mph (176kph).

Enthusiasts had been waiting, impatiently, for such a car for some years, and now that it was on the market they flocked to buy it. Even though it was not revealed until September 1963, no fewer than 848 of the new Sprint GT cars were produced before the year end (Bertone's body-manufacturing preparations had been completed well before launch day), and an amazing 10,839 cars followed in 1964. Right away, it seemed, the Sprint GT had made its mark for, as it was selling at the rate of more than 200 cars a week, this was already twice the best rate of sale ever achieved by the earlier Giulietta Sprint – and there was more to come.

In its Frankfurt Show report, *Autocar*'s reception of the new Sprint GT was very enthusiastic:

It is a two-door 2/4-seater and there is very reasonable accommodation, with headroom for adults in the rear compartment. The styling is an up-to-the-minute version of the elegant and ageless Giulietta introduced in 1954 with the American-inspired chamfered flanks, and single headlamps within the full-width grille ... Viewing the car from the side it appears that a last-minute decision was taken to shorten the wheelbase, for there is a big gap between the tyre and the back profile of the wheel arch. The body was styled by Bertone but it is to be made by Alfa Romeo in the new large factory at Arese ...

GTC Chop-Top

Touring made a brave attempt to produce a convertible version of the Giulia Sprint GT, dubbing it GTC. It worked well, but the shell was not stiff enough.

Soon after the Giulia Sprint GT was launched in 1963, Alfa Romeo decided to add a four-seater convertible to its range. Not wishing to tackle this on a production-line basis, it handed the job to an independent body builder, Carrozzeria Touring.

Starting with Giulia Sprint GT shells supplied from Milan, Touring produced a car to be badged the GTC (C = Cabriolet), eliminated the roof (and lost some stiffness in the process), but stiffened up the floorpan and understructure to compensate. Below the waistline, the Sprint GT's 'chassis', all the 1.6-litre running gear, the existing styling and the entire front-end plus doors, were retained, unchanged. Touring then arranged for new-type quarter windows to be retractable, to make this an entirely open car, and also designed their own fold-down soft-top.

A combination of a high price and a structure that was none too stiff meant that there was limited demand for the Guilia GTC: only 1,000 such cars were produced in 1964, 1965 and 1966. After this, the Pininfarina-styled Spider Duetto appeared and took its place.

The Touring-produced Giulia GTC provided dealers with a useful open-top car for two years, until the sensational new Duetto Spider arrived to elbow it aside.

When a new generation of cars goes on the market, first impressions are always important, and the new Giulia Sprint GT fared well. Everyone agreed that it looked beautiful and seemed to enjoy the handling, and there was never any argument about the performance. Not only that, but if the same lessons could be inferred from the old Giulietta's career, this was merely the first of what would be a large number of Sprint GT derivatives. And so it was. This might be a touch premature, but the following chart shows just how production of the mainstream family of Giulia cars based on this steel body would ebb and flow between 1963 and 1972:

Year	Giulia Sprint GT	Giulia Sprint GTC	Giulia Sprint GTV	Giulia GT1300 Junior	Giulia 1600 GTV
1963	848				
1964	10,839	106			
1965	10,053	600			
1966	162	292	7,201	3,176	
1967			6,541	13,020	
1968			29	12,732	
1969				15,674	
1970				13,694	
1971				15,359	
1972				6,968	4,495

In the meantime, the 1750 GTV had been launched in 1967, to be supplanted by the 2000 GTV in 1971.

This chart takes no account of the ultra-special aluminium-bodied versions (GTAs and GTA Juniors), nor of the Zagato-bodied 1300 and 1600 coupés which followed in the early 1970s.

In fact, by the end of 1972, with the life of Giulia-based cars by no means coming to an end, nearly 600,000 of all types of the Giulia family, along with 226,000 of the closely related 1750 and 2000 types, had already been built. Not bad for a company that had built only 162 cars in 1946, and only 3,321 in 1954, the year in which the original Giulietta had been launched!

For the next two years, Alfa Romeo's problem was not selling the Sprint GT, but satisfying the orders for these cars which flowed in from around the world. Customers for sporty cars, however, can be very fickle, and because the chassis was obviously capable of dealing with more, and there was a groundswell of demand for greater horsepower, the company set about developing a more powerful version – the Sprint GT Veloce.

Sprint GT Veloce

This new derivative was developed as a straight replacement for the Sprint GT. With the old Giulietta range, Sprint and Sprint Veloce models had been built in parallel for some years, but in this case there was to be absolutely no overlap. Only 162 Sprint GTs were built in the first weeks of 1966, before the Sprint GT Veloce took over completely.

The new car was unveiled rather modestly at the Geneva Motor Show in March 1966, where it was totally overshadowed in the publicity stakes by the launch of the Pininfarina-styled Giulia (Duetto) Spider, with which it shared the same

---

Duetto and Spider

Just as they had done with the Giulietta, Alfa Romeo made haste to approve a Pininfarina-styled and manufactured Spider version of the Giulia Sprint GTV. Completely different from the earlier variety, these Giulia-based Spiders ran on a shortened wheelbase (88.6in (2,250mm)) – even shorter than that of the Giulia Sprint GT – and were open-top two-seaters which shared the same front engine/rear drive running gear as the Sprint GTVs.

More rounded than the earlier Giulietta-based cars, these second-generation cars started life as 1,570cc-engined '1600 Duettos', but went on to have a long and quite remarkable career. Before the last was produced in 1993, well over 130,000 cars with various engines had been produced.

Along the way, the body shell was treated to a cropped tail from late 1970, and several other facelifts in the 1970s and 1980s; engines of 1,290cc, 1,570cc, 1,779cc and 1,964cc were employed, and power outputs varied from 89bhp to 132bhp.

The last of the Spiders, in fact, outlived its coupé equivalent by no less than seventeen years.

The Giulia Sprint GTV was announced in 1966, taking over from the original Sprint GT, with 109bhp and different gear ratios: a useful but not huge step forward. The grille, with three horizontal brightwork bars, was an easy recognition point.

uprated engine. There was in fact little that merited a great deal of hype, or even a relaunch, for the major changes made to the GT Veloce comprised a slightly more powerful and more torquey engine and a few noticeable, but not dramatic, style changes.

Although the engine was only boosted from 106bhp (DIN) at 6,000rpm to 109bhp (DIN) at 6,000rpm, and the peak torque had also been pushed up from 103lb ft at 3,000rpm to 105lb ft at 2,800rpm, the result was an engine that somehow felt more zestful than before. With an eye to the future and further expansion of the power unit, there were cylinder head porting changes, inlet valves had been enlarged from 35mm to 37mm, and there were changes to the camshaft profiles.

Visually, too, changes to the style and equipment were also minor. The front grille was retouched by the addition of three horizontal chrome strips between the headlamps and the shield, while there was also a new 'quadrifoglio'

(four-leaf clover) badge on the rear quarters at the base of the rear screen pillars, and a discreet 'Veloce' script on the tail.

The Sprint GTV was the first car in this family that I ever managed to drive (in 1964 and 1965, very few Sprint GTs ever came to Great Britain), my introduction taking place during a press facility trip arranged around Gardone and the blue waters of Lake Garda in northern Italy. My impressions, published in *Autocar*, remain with me to this day:

Power is delivered smoothly right up the scale, and over the top to 7,000rpm (explored briefly, and without distress); there seems to be no point at which surges or flat spots appear. Top speed, timed on the autostrada between kilometre posts, was about 115mph, while a couple of standing start sprints (two up) produced 0–60mph times of about 10.2sec. . . Though the steering is quite low geared, the handling is delicately balanced. The first wheel movement produces immediate response from the Pirelli Cinturatos fitted, and at most speeds there seems to be little understeer. On really tight bends or hairpins, the front seems to run wide, and inside rear wheel lift limits speeds at this point.

For a sporting car the suspension was rather soft; we would have preferred firmer dampers and a stiffer anti-roll bar to deal with this. Though the back axle is well located, by coil springs and radius arms, it jumps about quite a bit on rougher roads . . . Four large Dunlop discs, helped by a servo, make light work of the braking. Even several hard stops from 100mph on the autostrada produced no fade . . . The driving position, of course, is pure Italian. Seat back rake is adjustable, but a full arms-stretch position and straight legs are encouraged by the wheel and pedal layout.

That was my personal opinion, of course, but in the main my *Autocar* colleagues backed it up when they tested a right-hand-drive UK-market car towards the end of the 1966 season. Accurate measuring equipment put the top speed at 113mph (181kph), but it was perhaps more impressive that the (direct) fourth gear was good for exactly 100mph (160kph).

Know-alls who wondered why such an advanced-looking twin-cam engine could not develop more horsepower should perhaps have looked at the flexibility that Alfa's engineers had provided instead. In fourth gear, for instance, we found that the Sprint GTV would pull strongly and sweetly from less than 20mph (32kph), and that acceleration was then almost linear until 80mph (128kph) when wind resistance began to take a major effect.

Our summary told its own story:

> The trend today is towards closed GT coupés because for northern European weather they are much more practical. The stylist has more scope without the problems of folding the roof and usually he makes the car much more refined, comfortable and with that room in the back so essential to the family man . . . To have all this plus really brisk performance, compactness and handsome looks is much more rare. Add that indefinable quality that makes a car fun to drive and the list shortens considerably; the Alfa Giulia Sprint GTV has all this and more.

On the other side of the Atlantic, *Road & Track* waxed positively lyrical about the latest car's appeal:

> most staff members managed to find impeccable reasons either to renew their acquaintance or to see what they had missed three years ago. As testing proceeded, nearly every driver had praise for the car; a rather startling unanimity of opinion . . . the reasons for this broad spectrum of appeal are both simple and complex. They boil down to a machine carefully designed to become an extension of the human body, satisfying its wishes and amplifying its physical actions with a minimum of mechanical interference. This is no uncommon goal for automobile designers, of course, but the scarcity of such vehicles indicates the extreme difficulty of execution.

Here in Britain, in fact, as in most countries, the Giulia Sprint GTV's major problem lay in its price. Costing £1,950, it had to square up to the 140mph Jaguar E-Type 2+2 at £2,284, and it is worth noting that the original MG MGB GT, which was comfortably a 100mph (160kph) car with a similar seating package, sold for a mere £1,016.

There was little, in fact, that Alfa Romeo could do to reduce the price, for their running gear (which included the aluminium twin-cam engine and a five-speed transmission) was sophisticated and complex. The public, in any case, seemed to be happy enough to pay for such levels of performance and character – 6,901 were produced in 1966, and a further 6,541 in 1967 when this model was about to be replaced by the 1750 GT Veloce.

It was with the GTV, however, that Alfa Romeo truly laid the foundations of a long career for this range of cars. The company's expertise in the mix-and-match process of producing new models then kicked in, with exceptional results.

GT 1300 Junior

The last of the 1.3-litre-engined Giulietta Sprint coupés was built during 1965 (the last of the 1300 Spiders had already gone, in 1962), and for all

By the time the Giulia Sprint range was fully developed, there were engines from 1.3 litres to 2.0 litres. The GT 1300 Junior arrived in 1966, with its 89bhp/1,290cc engine and with a single horizontal brightwork stripe across the grille for recognition.

All Sprint GTs had generous 2+2 seating, this GT 1300 Junior showing the typical amount of space available.

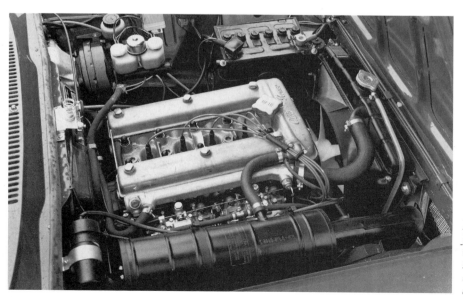

Although the GT 1300 Junior was the 'baby' of the range, its 1.3-litre engine still had twin horizontal dual-choke Weber carburettors.

The GT 1300 Junior's facia layout was typical of all the cars in this range, though in this case there was no console linking the facia with the transmission tunnel. Notice the floor-pivoting (not pendant) pedals.

manner of reasons (not least that it was easier to sell more-affordable 1.3-litre cars in countries where the fiscal regime favoured small engines) it was sorely missed. Alfa Romeo had recognized this and was already thinking ahead. In September 1966, therefore, a new derivative – the GT 1300 Junior – made its debut. This was the car, it was hoped, to crank up sporty Giulia coupé volumes to record levels.

As expected, it was a logical amalgam of Giulia GTV and old-style Giulietta engineering, further price reductions being assured by simplifying the trim and equipment specifications, but not the running gear. Visually, the only way to recognize the Junior was by seeing its simplified wheel trims, and the single horizontal brightwork stripe across the black mesh grille.

The engine was yet another updated derivative of the little twin-cam engine, this time with the familiar 1,290cc, still with twin horizontal dual-choke Weber carburettors, and now with 89bhp (DIN) at 6,000rpm. This was a specific output of 69bhp/litre, which was a remarkably high figure for those days.

To remind ourselves, the Giulietta 1300 Sprint had been fitted with an 80bhp engine and the Sprint Veloce with 90bhp, so this latest power unit was giving nothing away in the search for economy. Not only that, but the new 1300 Junior had the self-same five-speed gearbox and final drive ratios as the Giulia Sprint GTV, along with the same four-wheel disc brakes. Because it had to propel the heavier and bulkier Giulia Sprint GT shell, every bit of such power and transmission technology was welcome.

Alfa's master stroke, then, was to reduce the interior specification of the new car without making it look cheap and tacky. A simple type of three-spoke steering wheel (there were no alloy spokes until an upgrade in the early 1970s), rubber mats on the floor instead of carpets, and simpler and less-contoured front seats were typical.

All this helped Alfa to price the 1300 Junior well below the Sprint GTV: at its launch in September 1966, in its native Italy, it cost 1,695,000 lira instead of 2,245,000 lira, which was a massive 25 per cent reduction. And make no mistake, though this car was significantly slower than the sparkling GTV, it was by no means a gutless price-leader. Tests would later show that it could still beat 100mph (160kph), though in fairness no-one was very impressed by a 0–60mph time of 13.2 seconds.

The sales figures soon proved that the low-power/low-price gamble (if it had ever been so) had succeeded. Even though it was only officially on sale in the final four months of 1966, no fewer than 3,542 GT 1300 Juniors were made in that year, soaring to 13,020 in 1967 and 12,732 in 1968. It was already well on the way to becoming the best-selling model of all the cars marketed in this basic body style.

By 1969 the range had been reshuffled – the 1750 GT Veloce (*see* page 182) taking over as the flagship model – and the specification of the 1300 Junior had generally been upgraded to suit. In particular, there was now a proper alloy-spoked steering wheel, and (like the 1750 GT Veloce) the chassis ran on smaller, 165-14in tyres. Not only that, but there was now a diaphragm instead of a coil-spring clutch mechanism, the addition of a

---

GT 1300 Junior Z/1600 Junior Z (1969–72, 1972–75)

Layout

Unit-construction body-chassis structure, with steel and aluminium panels. Two-door, front engine/rear drive, sold as two-seater coupé model.

Engine

Block material	Cast aluminium
Head material	Cast aluminium
Cylinders	4 in-line
Cooling	Water
Main bearings	5
Valves	2 per cylinder, operated by twin-overhead camshafts and inverted bucket-type tappets, driven by chain from crankshaft

GT 1300 Junior Z, 1,290cc: bore and stroke 74 × 75mm; compression ratio 8.5:1; two horizontal twin-choke Weber 40DCOE28 carburettors; 89bhp (DIN) @ 6,000rpm, 101lb ft @ 3,200rpm

1600 Junior Z, 1,570cc: bore and stroke 78 × 82mm; compression ratio 9.0:1; two horizontal twin-choke Weber 40DCOE27 carburettors; 109bhp (DIN) @ 6,000rpm, 103lb ft @ 2,800rpm

Transmission

Five-speed all-synchromesh manual gearbox

Clutch	Single dry plate; hydraulically operated

Internal Gearbox Ratios

Top	0.86 (1300); 0.79 (1600)

GT 1300 Junior Z/1600 Junior Z (1969–72, 1972–75) *continued*

4th	1.00
3rd	1.355
2nd	1.988
1st	3.304
Reverse	3.010
Final drive	4.555:1

Suspension and Steering

Front	Independent, coil springs, wishbones, anti-roll bar, telescopic dampers
Rear	Live (beam) axle, by coil springs, radius arms, A-bracket, telescopic dampers, anti-roll bar
Steering	Recirculating ball, or worm and roller
Tyres	165–14in
Wheels	Steel disc, bolt-on
Rim width	4.5in

Brakes

Type	Disc brakes at front and rear, hydraulically operated
Size	10.5in front discs, 10.5in dia. rear discs

Dimensions

Track	
Front	52.2in (1,325mm)
Rear	50.2in (1,275mm)
Wheelbase	88.6in (2,250mm)
Overall length	153.5in (3,900mm)
Overall width	61.0in (1,550mm)
Overall height	50.4in (1,280mm)
Unladen weight	2,029lb (920kg) (1300); 2,095lb (950kg) (1600)

rear anti-roll bar, and an additional sound-deadening kit for the passenger compartment. Most noticeably, the GT Junior also got the new-style facia panel of the 1750 GT Veloce. Thus revived, the 1300 Junior continued to sell fast until 1972, when the 1600 Junior (*see* page 194) took over.

It is easy to see why the motoring world found this particular Alfa so attractive. Britain's *Autocar* tested an updated GT 1300 Junior in April 1969 (they then took it on to their staff fleet as a long-term test car), noting the simplified specification and the much reduced price, and concluding that: 'The GT Junior lacks only the sheer performance of the 1750. Compared with lesser cars, it offers unusually rapid, satisfying and inherently safe transport at a realistic price.'

A sporty Alfa, it seemed, did not have to rely on tyre-stripping performance to make friends.

1750 GT Veloce

In the meantime, the Sprint flagship had moved up another gear. First of all, in January 1968, Alfa Romeo introduced a newly styled 1750 saloon (which slotted into place above the Giulia saloon range, but relied heavily on that car for its platform and running gear) and, at the same time, revealed the Giulia 1750 GT Veloce coupé as a direct replacement for the Giulia Sprint GTV. So well organized was the company at this point that the first 919 of these new coupés had already been assembled before the end of 1967 – indeed, well over 1,000 such cars were built and on their way to the showrooms before introduction day.

When the 1750 GT Veloce appeared in 1967, it allowed Alfa Romeo and Bertone to smooth out the contours of the front wing/shroud/bonnet interface, this in fact being a GT Junior 1.6 with the revised metal shape which first appeared in 1972.

The 1750 GT Veloce had revised interior styling, the rear seating being shaped for only two people to sit alongside each other.

The 1750 GT Veloce not only had the new and somewhat smoother sheet metal shaping around the nose, but it also had four headlamps. The basic cabin, though, was not altered.

The 1750 GT Veloce instrument layout was familiar to all previous Sprint GT/GTV customers, but now had real wood on the panel, and a sturdy centre console.

In 1968, the classic coupé style of 1963 was improved further for the 1750 GT Veloce and later sister cars, not only by having four headlamps, but by running on 14in road wheels, too.

It would be easy, though misguided, to describe the new coupé as merely an up-engined Sprint GTV, for there was much more to it than this. The obvious changes included an enlarged, more powerful engine and a different front-end style, but there were other important improvements in the chassis, and in the equipment.

Once again, and without spending a fortune on new machine tooling, Alfa Romeo managed to enlarge the famous twin-cam engine by a valuable 13 per cent – from 1,570cc to 1,779cc. This was done, apparently modestly, not only by adding 2mm to the (wet-liner) cylinder bores, but by increasing the stroke from 82mm to 88.5mm. Alfa Romeo would maybe have liked to make a bigger increase to the cylinder bore dimensions, but because of the well-known space restrictions, this was barely possible. The result was that the '1750' was more of a long-stroke engine than before so, predictably, there was a bigger increase in torque than in peak power, as the following figures confirm:

Feature	1750 GT Veloce	Giulia Sprint GTV	Increase
Engine size	1,779cc	1,570cc	13 per cent
Peak power	122bhp/ 5,500rpm	109bhp/ 6,000rpm	12 per cent
Peak torque	127lb ft/ 2,900rpm	105lb ft/ 2,800rpm	21 per cent

1750 GT Veloce recognition points included four headlamps and a slightly different grille style.

1750 GT Veloce body shop assembly at Arese, near Milan, with rows of the famous coupés sharing space with the Giulia four-door saloon derivatives.

The quoted improvement in torque – a 21 per cent increment for only an 11 per cent increase in capacity – was so eyebrow-raising that some wondered if there had been some change in calibration measurements.

It was on this engine (for sale only in the USA, where their first tentative exhaust emission regulations were due to come into force in the 1968 calendar year) that Alfa Romeo's own SPICA fuel-injection system first appeared.

Behind the uprated engine was a newly developed diaphragm spring clutch (the first use of such equipment in the Giulia family), and although the five-speed gearbox itself was not changed, the propeller shaft was beefed up and given an increased diameter. The familiar suspension/braking installation was also modified. For the first time on these cars, the wheel diameter was reduced – from 15in to 14in – and the rim width went up (to 5.5in), which along with the addition of a rear anti-roll bar changed the suspension geometry enough to raise the roll centre a little and (Alfa claimed) cut the understeering tendency of this chassis. At the same time there were larger diameter front-wheel disc brakes, along with an ATE inertia-operated rear brake cut-off valve in the hydraulic lines.

The most obvious visual changes were to the nose and to the cabin. This was the first Giulia-based coupé to have four headlamps (this would never be donated to lesser-engined coupés). However, in consultation with stylist Giugiaro, Alfa also took the opportunity to rejig the front-end sheet metal. A side-by-side comparison with

1750 GT Veloces in the Arese body shop, this study showing the underside of the monocoque shell.

the original shape shows that the detailing of the nose was refined, for the 'step front' disappeared, as did the original layout of a bonnet panel which stood proud of the shroud panels. Inside the car there was now a smart new facia/instrument panel layout, with large speedometer and rev-counter dials standing proud from the facia itself, which along with a restyled centre console featured strips of real wood as opposed to the previous unsuitable plastic.

Less than three years after it had been announced – and ahead, as it happens, of the launch of yet another improved version of this popular coupé – there was a mid-life package of improvements: refinement changes to the engine, and a more stylish-looking trim package, including, for the first time, the option of cloth seating.

At this time I was a tester for *Autocar* magazine, one of a group who were avowed Alfa lovers; we all thought this car was a great improvement on

1750 GT Veloce assembly at Arese. This is what is often called 'body drop': you can see an engine/transmission assembly being threaded into the body of the car nearest the camera. Line upon line of similar engine/gearbox assemblies await their turn.

the 1.6-litre type, and noted that: 'Acceleration unchanged, but higher gearing and much less fuss; better economy. Excellent five-speed gearbox with well-matched ratios . . . Very expensive, but a most exhilarating and rewarding car to drive.'

And, in summary: 'We liked this little Alfa coupé when we tried it before as a 1,570, and many people regard its size as an ideal compromise, combining compactness with adequate seating for four adults. The extra engine capacity has made it more economical and although performance is not materially affected, the car is far more responsive and eager than before'.

Once again, this was to be a relatively short-lived model – Alfa Romeo believed in making regular changes to its cars – for the definitive 2000 GT Veloce would appear in mid-1971.

However, between 1968 and 1971, no fewer than 44,276 1750 GT Veloces were produced.

2000 GT Veloce

Less than four years after the 1750 models were launched, Alfa Romeo surprised even their greatest supporters by introducing a complete 2000 range to replace them. By pushing out the capacity of the now-legendary twin-cam engine from 1,779cc to 1,962cc, and bringing in further improvements to match, this rejuvenated an extremely successful model.

Alfa Romeo introduced a range of new 2000 saloons in a very logical way: coupés and Spiders were produced at the same time, because it was the running gear rather than the style and equipment that was being changed. The Arese factory, already busy as never before – well over 100,000 cars a year (2,000 every week, in other words) were being assembled – could best cope with simultaneous changes, rather than an untidy sequence of alterations to individual models.

The 2000 GT Veloce was the definitive Giulia-based coupé model, with 1,962cc instead of the 1,290cc with which this particular engine family had started life. Alfa had also found time to change the front-end (now with a horizontal emphasis to the grille backing the four headlamps), to provide yet another facia/instrument layout (all instruments were now closely grouped together, behind the steering wheel), to finalize

The 2000 GT Veloce appeared in 1971, to become the most powerful full series-production road-car version of this versatile model line. It had a 132bhp/2.0-litre engine and yet another grille.

The 2000 GT Veloce was in production from 1970 to 1977, and became the best-selling of all these types.

an air-conditioning installation, and to announce the option (fitted to a high proportion of the cars made) of a limited-slip differential.

Although the engine looked the same as before, the bore dimension had gone up from 80mm to 84mm, and many related internal changes had been made, none of them wrought without a great deal of effort. Because there was a space problem inside the cylinder block – repeated enlargement had already brought adjacent cylinder bores perilously close together –

any further increase in stroke was not practical, so yet another bore increase would have to be accomplished.

It was Charles Bulmer, *Motor*'s distinguished Editor, who described the changes so succinctly at the time:

The problem of enlargement had already been solved for the GT/Am cars, such as the one in which Toine Hezemans won the 1970 European Saloon Championship: the method adopted was to cast the four

Although not 'homologation specials', the 2000 GT Veloces were competitive where Group 1 or 'standard car' regulations applied, this being Stan Clark driving one of his dealership's machines in the 1973 Tour of Britain.

cylinder liners as a single unit so that the separation between adjacent bores need be no more than the thickness of a single liner wall instead of two. This cylinder unit is then dropped into the light alloy cylinder block . . . However, to keep the engine smooth and reliable, it then proved necessary to enlarge the five main bearings of the crankshaft (but not the big end bearings), and also to modify the water flow in the cylinder block . . . So, all in all, providing the engine with bigger holes has demanded a very extensive redesign.'

These extensive changes, made primarily to ben-

efit the 2000 saloon, but obviously valuable on the coupé, provided the highest and final engine tune achieved on this range of cars:

Feature	2000 GT Veloce	1750 GT Veloce	Increase
Engine size	1,962cc	1,779cc	10 per cent
Peak power	132bhp/ 5,500rpm	122bhp/ 5,500rpm	8 per cent
Peak torque	134lb ft/ 3,000rpm	127lb ft/ 2,900rpm	5.5 per cent

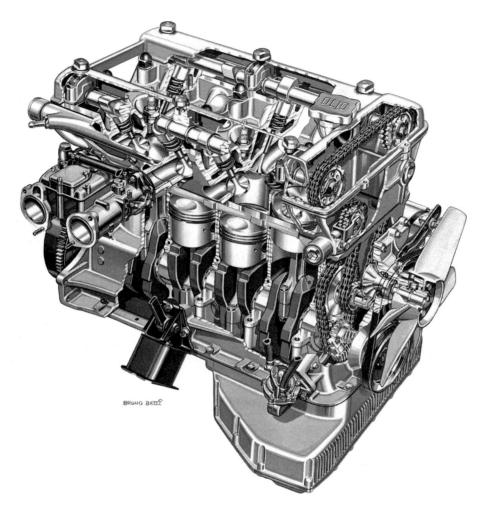

The 1,962cc version of this engine reached the limit of capacity, with a cylinder bore of 84mm, and virtually no space for water between the cylinder bores.

BRUNO BELL

In many testers' eyes, the 2000 GT Veloce was now the car it should have been for some time – faster, better-equipped and more sure-footed. It was *Autocar*'s road-test headline which summarized the car's charm: 'Same style, more punch'. A glowing report that went on to list a 120mph (193kph) top speed, 0–60mph in 9.2 seconds, and an overall (hard-driven) fuel consumption of 21.1 mpg, along with the following:

> In a world which usually dictates that the more stylish an object, the more frequently it needs changing, the Alfa GTV has been a refreshing exception ... With the 2000 engine, the GTV moves into the perform-

ance class many customers expect of it: it is now a genuinely quick car with relaxed 100-110mph cruising capacity. Alfa's efforts of recent years to improve detail and overall finish show to advantage: the car is a really attractive package ... As always, the real attraction of the car is its feeling of precision and responsiveness: the extra power seems to have added to this without detracting from anything.

The good news, too, was that the limited-slip differential option seemed to work really well:

> The 2000 GTV's handling is brought even closer to racing – rather than rally – car characteristics by the

This was the final version of the facia layout, as seen in the 2000 GT Veloce of 1971, still recognizably evolved from that of the original Giulia Sprint GT of 1963.

fitting of a limited-slip differential. The car goes exactly where it is put in any corner, and applying more or less power hardly changes the line at all . . . With the limited-slip differential coming into play, traction is much improved, and far more power can be used much earlier. This permits a higher cornering speed …

Demand for this car, need I say, was always extremely healthy – no fewer than 12,134 were produced in the first full year (1972) – and was robust until 1975, when a more modern Alfa coupé (the Alfetta GT: *see* Chapter 6) was freely available. Even so, this model stayed in production until 1976, when the last of no fewer than 37,459 2000 GT Veloces were finally assembled.

GT 1600 Junior

The final phase of Giulia-based coupé development was unveiled in mid-1972, when Alfa Romeo launched a GT 1600 Junior, which was really no more and no less than a two-headlamp GT 1300 Junior but with the larger and more powerful 1,570cc engine. It was also, if you care to think of it in this way, a reversion to the power train of the 1966-type Sprint GT Veloce, for the engine was similarly rated and the performance was the same.

From mid-1974 there was another change to this model, in which the engine was slightly derated (to 102bhp), and the four-headlamp nose of the 2000 GT Veloce, and much of the plush interior, was adopted to rationalize the production process, though the limited-slip differential was never available on this entry-level model.

And so it was that the thirteen-year life of this remarkable coupé came to an end, with more than 210,000 of all types and derivatives assembled at Arese in that time. Because it had no internal competition, the coupé's near relative, the Pininfarina-styled Spider, would remain on the market for another seventeen years, until 1993, but now was the time for the coupé to give way to the already-launched Alfetta GT models, which shared the same twin-cam engines but were otherwise totally different.

Alfa Romeo Giulia GT Family Performance

This is a summary of the figures achieved by Britain's most authoritative magazine, *Autocar*, of cars supplied for test over the years:

Model	Giulia GT1300 Junior	Giulia Sprint GTV	Giulia 1750 GT Veloce	Giulia 2000 GTV
	1,290cc 89bhp	1,570cc 109bhp	1,779cc 122bhp	1,962cc 131bhp
Max. speed (mph)	102	113	116	120
Acceleration (sec):				
0–60mph	13.2	11.1	11.2	9.2
0–80mph	25.3	19.2	19.0	16.2
0–100mph	–	35.4	36.9	27.7
Standing 1/4-mile (sec)	19.1	17.7	18.0	16.4
Consumption (mpg)				
Overall	24.4	21.9	23.9	21.1
Typical	27	25	25	23
Kerb weight (lb (kg))	2,224 (1,015)	2,286 (1,037)	2,240 (1,020)	2,301 (1,044)
Year tested	1969	1966	1968	1972
Tested by	*Autocar*	*Autocar*	*Autocar*	*Autocar*

5 TZ, GTA and Zagato Coupés – Not Forgetting the Montreal

Despite the fact that Alfa Romeo rarely made any money, and that a financial expert would say that they really should have concentrated on making more ordinary cars to pay the rent, that simply wasn't Alfa's way of doing things.

In the 1950s, they had indulged themselves in Grand Prix racing with the Alfetta race cars, then followed up with the fierce racing sports machines and the splendid little SZs. But that was then; now there was a future to consider. In the 1960s and the 1970s, they would carry on with the same enthusiasm but with new products.

This, in many ways, was one of Alfa's most pro-ductive periods. First there was the amazing TZ two-seater, then the GTA (which looked like a Giulia Sprint GT Veloce, but wasn't), and after that there was time to revert to pure racing cars like the Tipo 33s. Oh yes, and Zagato was encouraged to build yet another variation of coupé-style Giulia, for road use.

Tubolare Zagato – a Fast Little Race Car

I was always a great fan of the Giulia TZ, which achieved great things in sports car racing, and

The fabulously complex Giulia TZ which, complete with a multi-tube frame and all-independent suspension, was about as different from the Giulia as was possible. Only 124 such cars were ever built.

Above *Bertone's style for the Giulietta Sprint and Sprint Veloce coupés caused a sensation when it was unveiled in the mid-1950s. Nothing so sleek, functional and beautiful had ever before been seen on such a compact base.*

Right *The Giulietta Sprint and Sprint Veloce style was so carefully detailed that it looked sporty and purposeful from every angle. Only the badging — on the flanks and on the boot lid — tell us that this is the higher-powered Sprint Veloce version.*

Every detail of the Sprint-bodied Giulietta looked right — and from every angle too. Nothing superfluous, nothing out of place and nothing missing. You couldn't confuse a Giulietta with any other car.

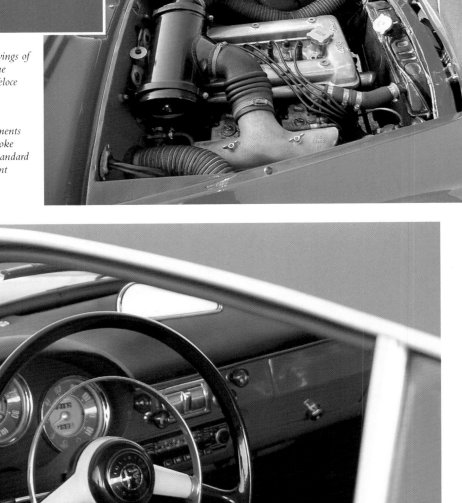

Above *The script on the front wings of this Giulietta tells us that it is the higher-powered, 90bhp, Sprint Veloce type.*

Right *Rather convoluted inlet trunking and air cleaner arrangements hide the twin horizontal dual-choke Weber carburettors, which were standard equipment on the Giulietta Sprint Veloce.*

Purposeful, nicely detailed, and well-equipped: the facia/instrument panel of the Giulietta Sprint Veloce.

Above When Zagato set out to build the ultimate high-
performance Giulietta, the style of the SZ was wrapped as
tightly around the shortened wheelbase of the coupé's platform as
possible. At the same time it was curvaceous and wickedly
attractive. The Campagnolo alloy wheels were extras.

Right Shorter than the standard Sprint, with very basically
trimmed two-seater accommodation, the Giulietta SZ was a no-
excuses little competition car. Gorgeous!

Below Many art lovers reckon that the Giulietta SZ was the prettiest of all Alfa coupés, for it was at once sexy and functional, stylish
and effective. The optional Campagnolo road wheels add to the effect. Yet only 200 such cars were built.

Above *Best not to have an accident in your Giulietta SZ, as this rear-end study makes clear: not only were there no bumpers, but the body shell itself was as light as possible. But who cares? It was a stunningly effective competition car.*

Giulietta SZs were built for motor racing, not for comfort, which explains the simple layout of the instruments, controls and seats of this car. The full-harness belts prove that it is still used in speed events, to this day. After all, this particular car started six successive Targa Florio races in the 1960s!

Except for the Giulia GTA-type carburettor air trumpets and GTA oil filler, this SZ engine is almost exactly as Conrero intended it in the late 1950s. An output of 100bhp from 1.3 litres was phenomenal for this period of Alfa history.

Above *The Giulia Sprint GT family started life as a 1.6-litre car in 1963, and ended it as a much-changed 2-litre model in the 1970s, selling in big quantities. This 1750GTV of the late 1960s is typical of that timeless 2+2-seater shape by Bertone. This French Blue car was built in 1969, during the transition period between what are known as 'Mk 1' and 'Mk 2' versions, which explains the Mk 1 equipment, but the later Mk 2 colour and tail lamps. Four headlamps and the smooth-panel nose were novelties in the 1750GTV.*

Right *By the late 1960s, Alfa Romeo had taken notice of the way its cars were selling in export markets. This, perhaps, explains why its sporting coupés had much more completely equipped interiors than ever before.*

Left *Although the Giulia/1750GTV/ 2000GTV package was virtually the same size as that of the earlier Giuliettas, the cabin was much more spacious. From this three-quarter rear angle, the location of the rear seats and the size of the boot are obvious. Bertone, of course, had done yet another superb job, in making this a quite unmistakeable sporting Alfa. The door mirrors were an optional extra.*

Giugiaro's style on the Alfetta GT platform was a triumph in every way. The Alfetta saloon, on which this car was based, was undistinguished, but the coupé was beautifully detailed and masculine in its character, yet still found space for four passengers. By the time this V6-engined version came along the front-end had been retouched, and of course there was a bonnet bulge to accommodate the bulky engine.

The Alfetta GTV 2.5 combined the best of Giugiaro's Alfetta style, with the lusty power and torque of the new V6 engine, the most spine-chilling engine noises and great character.

With this sporty version of the Alfetta, Giugiaro's genius was to produce a beautiful fastback/hatchback style, yet still leave space for a four-seater interior. The cast alloy road wheels were a nice touch, and the under-front-bumper spoiler was strictly functional.

First seen in the Alfa Six saloon, which was a very ordinary car indeed, the new 60-degree V6 became one of the best engines ever to find use in a sporting Alfa Romeo. This was the original Alfetta GTV 2.5 installation of the early 1980s; twenty years later, with many updates, it was still a well-loved engine.

Alfa Romeo always got its details right, such as the use of the famous badge in the centre of the Alfetta GTV 2.5's alloy road wheels.

Probably one of the most famous badges in the world! The Alfa Romeo badge, and the 1980s-version of the 'shield' grille, meant that every enthusiast in the world knew what he was admiring.

The most controversial feature of the original Alfetta GTV, and the V6-engined version that followed it, was the instrument display, which placed the speedometer in a separate pod, ahead of the driver's eyes. Many customers would have preferred to have the rev-counter there instead.

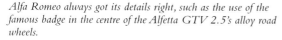

In some ways, the Alfasud Sprint was a 'baby brother' version of the larger Alfetta GTV, for there were many similarities in the proportions.

It is never easy to make a front-wheel-drive coupé look pretty, but Alfa Romeo achieved it, splendidly, with the Sud Sprint. The use of a low, flat-four engine helped a lot.

By the time this Sud Sprint Veloce was put on sale, the flat-four's engine size had been pushed up to 1.5 litres, and the smart little car could easily exceed 100mph (160km/h), with secure, front-wheel-drive chassis handling.

Because the engine of the Sud Sprint Veloce was a flat-four, mounted ahead of the line of the front wheels, it was almost hidden away under the air cleaner and fuel supply arrangements of this car. Not much of the car's package, therefore, was taken up by the 'oily bits'.

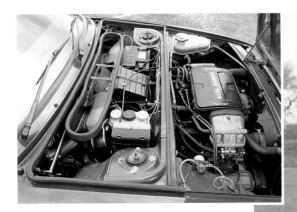

Right Every student of automotive design should study the styling details of Alfa Romeos. Here, at the front of a Sud Sprint Veloce, twin headlamps, a front spoiler, a turn indicator and an energy-absorbing bumper are neatly blended, without a blemish.

This, in theory, is a Giulia TZ road car of 1963, though when did you ever see a TZ with nave plates on the wheels, or looking as if it was going down to the shops? In racing form, with 170bhp from its 1.6-litre engine, it was a formidable race car.

even in tarmac rallying. With its complicated multi-tube chassis and its fragile light-alloy body, it was the sort of project that only a petrol-head outfit like Alfa Romeo would ever consider. Alfa would eventually call it a derivative of the 'Giulia', but the links were tenuous. Except for the same basic engine and gearbox, it was not even closely related, for the chassis, suspension and the body shell were all unique.

As a motor racing project – with the lightest and most purposeful structure that could be wrapped around the newly developed 1.6-litre version of the twin-cam engine – it was right, and absolutely in focus. It was the natural successor for the splendid little Giulietta SZ, a better car in every way.

And why? Because right at the heart of Alfa Romeo there was always an urge to go motor racing, an urge to compete at the highest level, and an urge to be flamboyant, successful, and to enjoy itself in every possible way. Denied the chance to go back into Grand Prix racing, the company set out to make the best possible racing two-seater that its engineers could devise. The brief was simple enough. The stubby little Giulietta SZ needed to be replaced by something better – and faster. With similar links between Zagato, engine-tuner Conrero and Alfa's engineers, it was a wonderful challenge.

Even though its launch was long delayed – design had begun in 1959, though it was not launched until 1963 – the TZ was always an advanced car. There were several technical influences, most notably the multi-tube spaceframe chassis which Mercedes-Benz and Lotus had made so effective in the 1950s, the lightweight

Giulia TZ (Tubolare Zagato) (1963–67)

Layout

Multi-tubular chassis frame, covered by two-seater body shell, with steel and aluminium panels. Two-door, front engine/rear drive, sold as two-seater competition coupé model.

Engine

Block material	Cast aluminium
Head material	Cast aluminium
Cylinders	4 in-line
Cooling	Water
Bore and stroke	78 × 82mm
Capacity	1,570cc
Main bearings	5
Valves	2 per cylinder, operated by twin-overhead camshafts and inverted bucket-type tappets, driven by chain from crankshaft
Compression ratio	9.7:1
Carburation	Two horizontal twin-choke Webers 45DCOE 14 carburettors
Max. power	112bhp (DIN) @ 6,500rpm
Max. torque	112lb ft @ 4,200rpm

Transmission

Five-speed all-synchromesh manual gearbox

Clutch	Single dry plate; hydraulically operated

Internal Gearbox Ratios

Top	0.85
4th	1.00
3rd	1.355
2nd	1.988
1st	3.26
Reverse	3.25
Final drive	4.1:1, 4.555:1 or 5.125:1, to choice

Suspension and Steering

Front	Independent, coil springs, wishbones, anti-roll bar, telescopic dampers
Rear	Independent, coil springs, wishbones, radius arms, telescopic dampers, anti-roll bar
Steering	Worm and roller
Tyres	155–15 radial-ply
Wheels	Steel disc, bolt-on
Rim width	4.5in

Brakes

Type	Disc brakes at front and rear, hydraulically operated
Size	11.2in front discs, 11.5in dia. rear discs

Dimensions

Track	
Front	51.2in (1,300mm)
Rear	51.2in (1,300mm)
Wheelbase	86.7in (2,200mm)
Overall length	155.5in (3,950mm)
Overall width	59.4in (1,510mm)
Overall height	47.2in (1,200mm)
Unladen weight	1,455lb (660kg)

body-style construction from Zagato, and input from Delta Automobili (which soon became Autodelta), who would complete the production cars.

The spaceframe – albeit a not-particularly scientifically designed spaceframe – was used simply to get the weight down. The 1.3-litre-engined SZ had always been an effective little car, but even when thoroughly stripped out, it still weighed in at about 1,698lb (770kg), which was a bit too solid for it to challenge more specialized machinery like the Abarths, Porsches and (increasingly) the Alpine-Renaults.

Because the SZ had been based on a short-wheelbase version of the Giulietta road car's platform – a sturdy pressed-steel structure – there was a limit to what could be saved. For a replacement car, the new Giulia's platform could have been used, but that had an even more substantial steel platform and was still lumbered with a beam axle rear suspension, and the engineers wanted to better it.

The result was that the project leader – Edo Mazoni of Alfa's own design staff – chose to go for a multi-tube frame, which saved 242lb (110kg). You only have to compare their official power/weight ratios of fully race-prepared race cars to see that it worked:

Giulietta SZ	182 bhp/tonne
Giulia TZ	257 bhp/tonne

A greatly encouraging improvement of no less than 41 per cent.

Technicalities

Because the new car took shape around a multi-tubular frame, and the body would be styled and manufactured by Zagato, the choice of a title – TZ – was logical enough, as this stood for 'Tubolare Zagato' (Tubular, Zagato).

The original Giulietta SZ had always been a stubby but effective little jewel of a car (final versions, though, had featured longer nose/longer tail versions of the same shape), yet the larger-engined TZ had an even shorter wheelbase but a slightly elongated shape, and weighed less. The following is an immediate comparison:

Dimension	Giulietta SZ	Giulia TZ
Wheelbase	88.6in (2,250mm)	86.7in (2,200mm)
Front track	50.9in (1,292mm)	51.2in (1,300mm)
Overall length	149.6in (3,799mm)	155.5in (3,950mm)
Overall width	61.0in (1,549mm)	59.4in (1,510mm)
Overall height	48.0in (1,219mm)	47.2in (1,200mm)
Unladen weight	1,698lb (770kg)	1,455lb (660kg)

According to aeronautical experience (where multi-tube frame design had originated and come to maturity), groups of tubes should spring from high-stress key points – such as the top of the suspension mountings, the rear axle mountings, and main bulkhead/floor areas – and all stresses should be taken in tension or compression, but never in torsion or bending. In an ideal technical world, this should make little allowance for access to the engine, or even to the passenger cabin!

However, as Mercedes-Benz had found out with the famous 'gull-wing' 300SL, for a car to be habitable this could never properly be achieved. They, and Alfa Romeo, had to settle for severely compromised layouts. Accordingly, the multi-tube undersill longeron sections were quite shallow, while those wrapping around the engine were perhaps not as deep as theory would suggest.

In later years Alfa Romeo admitted that the position and number of the small-diameter tubes evolved partly through applied science, and partly through testing. At one stage, a prototype frame was pinned to workshop fixtures at three corners, and weights added to the free-standing fourth corner, so that the tendency of the frame to twist could then be assessed. If and where the deflection was too high, either a larger diameter tube or an extra bit of bracing would be added to rectify this. In the end, the bare multi-tubular chassis weighed a mere 88lb (40kg), which represented a huge saving over using the platform of a road car, no matter how carefully that could be pared down to size.

In 'base', or standard form, the engine was a 112bhp version of the Giulia's new 1,570cc twin-cam, exactly the same as that already being supplied in the Giulia Sprint Speciale (and in the Giulia TI Super saloon 'homologation special', which went on sale at about the same time), this being matched by a version of the five-speed transmission which was becoming standard on all the mid-size Alfas. In race-prepared guise, up to 170 reliable bhp (at 7,500rpm, with a rev limit of 8,000rpm) was available.

The engine itself was set well back in the tubular frame – the front of the engine was behind the line of the front 'axle' – and for packaging reasons, to provide enough space for the twin dual-choke Weber carburettors on the right side of the engine bay, it was canted slightly over towards the left of the car.

Independent suspension by coil springs and locating links – using mainly tubular links – was used all round, with four-wheel disc brakes (the SZ had used drums), this being the very first time such a system had been offered on an Alfa 'road car'. At the front there were coil springs, upper and lower wishbones, separately positioned telescopic dampers, and an anti-roll bar, which was simple and predictable enough.

It was at the rear where the complications – and a great deal of grief at the development stage – appeared. The suspension was in the form of a Chapman-strut layout, with coil-over-shocks units, fixed-length drive shafts, lower wishbones and radius arms, plus an anti-roll bar and the ability to change ride heights and toe-in/toe-out settings. For a time, it seems, this rear suspension simply did not work as well as that of the existing Giulietta SZ (which had a solid rear axle), which partly explains the considerable delay in getting the TZ from 'good idea' to 'public launch', and on to 'available for delivery'.

Aside from the fact that Alfa Romeo's top bosses had to approve it, the style itself was not influenced from the factory, but was pure Zagato, and was a definite evolution of that of the two phases of SZ. Original SZs had been short and rounded little cars, whereas the final SZs were longer at the nose, longer at the tail, with an enlarged rear window and with a 'Kamm'-type cut-off tail panel.

Even though it still had to be a minimum-size two-seater, where motorsport and function took precedence over all other fripperies, the TZ took that process a stage further. Although longer than the SZ, it was slightly lower and narrower. This time, however, it had a three-piece rear window, the combination of low roof and high cut-off tail ensuring that it was almost horizontal. The shell itself, ultra-light and not really practical for the hurly-burly of everyday heavy traffic usage, was made almost entirely from thin-gauge aluminium panels, with perspex instead of glass for some of the windows, the large flat rear panel always being painted in matt black. The entire front end/front wings/bonnet was one assembly, hinged in the nose, and could be swivelled up for access to the engine bay. The famous Alfa front grille, of course, was on the nose, but there were no bumpers. Like the SZ before it, the TZ would have looked odd with any such form of chrome protection. Inside the car, the trim was simple, not to say stark, with an instrument display dominated by the large rev-counter.

The very first TZ to be shown in public – at the Turin Motor Show in November 1962 – featured a pair of large, rectangular headlamps hidden behind glass fairings. These were not liked – frankly they did not seem to suit the curvaceous style – and were speedily abandoned.

Career

When previewed in Turin, the new car was placed on the Zagato stand (not the main Alfa display), was called 'GTZ', and was supposedly to be made available for 1963 in 1,290cc and 1,570cc-engined form. The name change, and the decision to concentrate on the larger-engined type, came about before deliveries actually began.

Although prototype testing had begun in 1961 (admittedly there was a great deal of trouble in getting the rear suspension to work properly, and to ensure that the tubular chassis was stiff enough), there were delays in making cars available for sale. Officially, Alfa Romeo insisted that this was because they had to concentrate on the launch of the mainstream Giulias and 2600 models, but this was a rather obfuscatory remark which didn't ring true.

Just 100 cars had to be built to make this car eligible for Appendix J Group 3 International sports car racing, and although this number seems to be quite small in absolute terms, the choice of the multi-tube frame meant that it was still an awkward one for Alfa Romeo to consider making itself. In the end, manufacture of the entire car was farmed out, the project centring on a newly maturing company, Delta Automobili, and this is where the notable figure of Carlo Chiti enters the Alfa Romeo story. Having designed Ferrari's famous shark-nose F1 car of 1961, and

---

Carlo Chiti (1924–94)

The engineer who finally convinced Ferrari to adopt mid-engined race car layouts played an important role in Alfa Romeo's sporting success in the 1960s and 1970s.

Chiti started his career with Alfa Romeo after graduating in aeronautical engineering. Having moved to Ferrari at Maranello, he finally gained Enzo Ferrari's approval to design a new mid-engined 1.5-litre F1 car, which proved to be all-conquering in 1961. Then, after a blazing row with Ferrari, he moved to set up the ATS F1 project, which failed dismally.

After setting up Autodelta in Udine – close to the border with Yugoslavia – he joined forces with Alfa Romeo, moved his business much closer to Milan (to Settimo Milanese) from 1964, and effectively became Alfa's 'works' motorsport operation, not only running race cars, but building machines like the Type 33, and an amazing variety of F1 engines.

Having split with Alfa Romeo in 1984, he then set up Motori Moderni, which supplied several turbocharged F1 engines, but he had left his best days behind him.

Autodelta + Alfa Romeo, however, was a formidable combination.

---

fresh from the commercial disaster of the ATS project of 1962, he had set up a new tuning business along with Ludovico Chizzola, and was looking for work.

Almost immediately he made contact with Alfa Romeo, who admired his record, turned his company into Autodelta, and began a long and fruitful relationship with the Milanese concern. Alfa therefore contracted out almost all the realization of the TZ project. It would provide engine/transmission and other running gear pieces, Zagato would manufacture the coupé bodies, while Autodelta would manufacture the chassis and then assemble the complete cars. Not only that, but Autodelta would also be responsible for power tuning the engines for race cars, and for the operation of the 'works' competition cars.

Although this might have sounded optimistic, it was an arrangement that actually worked very well – and would carry on working very well for many years to come.

The first examples of the Tubolare Zagato (TZ) were ready for delivery in 1963, and although in theory there was a road car version of this car – priced at 3.7 million lira (approximately £1,850 at 1963 currency rates, and therefore about twice the retail price of a Ford Lotus-Cortina) – with glass wind-up door windows and something approaching complete interior trim, the vast majority of all TZs were prepared with motorsport in mind.

To become eligible for sports car racing, 100 'identical' cars had to be produced, and even though series production of TZs was well underway by the summer of 1963, it is highly unlikely that so many cars were produced before homologation was achieved later in the year. In the end, Alfa claimed to have built just 112 TZs (or, as they later became known, TZ1s), most of those cars being completed at Autodelta in 1963 and 1964. Available thereafter, they were no longer in demand when the more versatile (and cheaper) Giulia GTA came along in 1965, so Autodelta then contented itself by building a further twelve TZ2s.

These had the same basic chassis (with some development tweaks around the suspension), but were fitted with an even lower and more purposeful body in glassfibre, once again styled and produced by Zagato. The last cars, too, could be fitted with a twin-spark version of the engine, which made its debut in the GTA in 1965.

The ultimate TZ was the lower and even more specialized GRP-bodied TZ2, as driven here by Richard Pilkington in a British club event.

Although the TZ was not a great road car – the ride was hard, comforts were sparse, and the interior could get unbearably hot when the engine was working hard – from 1963 to 1965 it was an extremely successful competition car. Not only did it go like the wind, but it looked gorgeous (comparisons with the Ferrari GTO were often made), and when pushed really hard with open exhausts it made the most spine-tingling noises.

Because it had to wait until sporting homologation was achieved, the race programme did not begin until the end of the 1963 season, but the TZ then made a promising start by winning its class in a Monza sports car race. Then, in 1964, when endurance and hour-in, hour-out reliability counted for so much, it dominated its 1.6-litre class – at Sebring, in the Tour de France, in the Targa Florio (plus third and fourth overall), in the Nurburgring 1000km and in the Le Mans 24 hour race.

Even in standard 112bhp form, a TZ was good for at least 130mph (209kph), but in race tune (and

TZs were rare, but TZ2s like this, complete with ultra-low styling and GRP body panels, were almost mythical. Only twelve were ever produced – all of them for circuit racing.

A TZ2, hard at racing work in 1966. It was no coincidence, surely, that Zagato leaned towards the style of the Ferrari GTO when shaping this second-evolution TZ in 1965.

The rear view of one of the twelve Giulia TZ2s produced by Autodelta from 1965 to 1967.

depending on the gearing employed) it could reach 155–160mph (249–257kph). For a 1.6-litre machine this was magnificent, and goes a long way to explain why one of these cars lapped the Le Mans circuit at more than 112mph (180kph).

Achievements in true long-distance events – like the ten-day Tour de France and the five-day open-road French Alpine rally – were even more startling. In the Alpine Rally – a mixture of hundreds of open-road miles, speed hillclimbs and special stages – Frenchman Jean Rolland's TZ won the entire event outright; not merely its class, but outright, defeating Porsche 904GTs and the fearsome 'works' Austin-Healey 3000s in the process. In the Tour de France, the same car/driver combination easily won its 1.6-litre class, finishing seventh overall in the GT category, behind two Ferraris and four 2-litre Porsche 904s.

Motorsport, however, was moving swiftly on in the mid-1960s, and because Alfa was already looking ahead for outright victories, it wanted a fresh category to conquer, which is where, and why, the Giulia GTA came on to the scene.

Giulia GTA – Alfa's Amazing 'Touring Car'

A touring car? But surely this book is about coupés?

The Giulia GTA was indeed a coupé, yet Alfa Romeo also persuaded the sport's governing body that it was a full four-seater which qualified as a 'saloon car'. This explains why the GTA (and its lineal development, the GTAm) spent most of its time racing against Ford Lotus-Cortinas, Lancias and BMW 1800TiSAs!

Announced in 1965, the Giulia GTA was a serious attempt to match the Ford Lotus-Cortina in motorsport. Not only did it have twin-spark ignition, but it was considerably lighter than the GTV.

The GTA's facia/instrument layout was functional rather than glitzy, for there were lightweight rubber mats on the floor, a simple wood-rimmed steering wheel, and a rev-counter not red-lined until 6,750rpm was reached.

Giulia GTA range (1965–72, all types)

(Note: the 1750 GTAm and 2000 GTAm models were not production cars, but were built purely for racing by Autodelta in 1970 and 1971)

Layout

Unit-construction body-chassis structure, with steel structure, and many aluminium skin panels. Two-door, front engine/rear drive, sold as 2+2-seater coupé model.

Engine

Block material	Cast aluminium
Head material	Cast aluminium
Cylinders	4 in-line
Cooling	Water
Main bearings	5
Valves	2 per cylinder, operated by twin-overhead camshafts and inverted bucket-type tappets, driven by chain from crankshaft

GTA 1300 Junior, 1,290cc (1968–72): bore and stroke 74 × 75mm; compression ratio 9.0:1; two horizontal twin-choke Weber 45DCOE14 carburettors; 96bhp (DIN) @ 6,000rpm, 96lb ft @ 5,000rpm

GTA, 1,570cc (1965–69): bore and stroke 78 × 82mm; compression ratio 9.7:1; two horizontal twin-choke Weber 45DCOE14 carburettors; 115bhp (DIN) @ 6,000rpm, 119lb ft @ 5,500rpm

Transmission

Five-speed all-synchromesh manual gearbox

Clutch	Single dry plate; hydraulically operated

Internal Gearbox Ratios

GTA 1600

Top	0.791
4th	1.00
3rd	1.355
2nd	1.988
1st	3.304
Reverse	3.010
Final drive	4.555:1

GTA 1300

Top	0.791
4th	1.00
3rd	1.26
2nd	1.70
1st	2.54
Reverse	3.010
Final drive	4.555:1

Other sets of gear ratios and final drive ratios were available as optional extras.

Suspension and Steering

Front	Independent, coil springs, wishbones, anti-roll bar, telescopic dampers
Rear	Live (beam) axle, by coil springs, radius arms, A-bracket, telescopic dampers. Anti-roll bar on GTA 1300
Steering	Recirculating ball, or worm and roller
Tyres	155–15 radial-ply (GTA 1600); 165HR–14 (GTA 1300)
Wheels	Cast alloy disc, bolt-on
Rim width	4.5in (GTA 1600 and GTA 1300)

Brakes

Type	Disc brakes at front and rear, hydraulically operated
Size	10.5in front discs, 9.75in dia. rear discs (GTA 1600)
	(10.5in dia. rear discs on GTA 1300)

Dimensions

Track	
Front	51.5in (1,310mm); 52.1in (1,324mm) (GTA 1300)
Rear	50.1in (1,270mm)
Wheelbase	92.5in (2,350mm)
Overall length	160.5in (4,080mm)
Overall width	62.2in (1,580mm)
Overall height	51.7in (1,315mm)
Unladen weight	1,641lb (745kg) (GTA 1600); 1,674lb (760kg) (GTA 1300)

Giulia GTAs were extremely successful on the race track and in rallying, for they were very fast and very nimble. This was the De Adamich/Galli example, on its way to fourth overall in a Touring Car race at the Nurburgring in 1967.

One of my favourite GTA occasions came in 1966, when I saw Frenchman Jean Rolland winning the French Alpine rally outright, beating the might of the Ford, BMC and Renault 'works' teams.

Up to that point, Alfa's early-1960s saloon car racer was the Giulia Ti Super, which was really too heavy and not aerodynamically 'slippery' enough, so a better version was needed. Here was a case where the regulations came first, and the GTA evolved to meet them. A car could be homologated for saloon car racing under Appendix J Group 2 rules if the makers could produce 1,000 cars, and if they could prove that these were four-seater machines that complied with certain minimum cabin dimensions.

Like other sporting-minded car-makers, Alfa Romeo was resourceful. Reasoning that achieving the minimum cabin dimensions was not too demanding (if a Mini-Cooper could get through them, surely a Giulia Sprint GT could do the same?), especially if the rear seats of cars to be measured just happened to have very thin, uncomfortable cushions and backrests. They decided to match the opposition.

Dimensions were one thing; idealizing a new version of the Giulia Sprint GT to make it more competitive in motorsport was quite another. Having seen what other manufacturers – notably Ford, with its new Lotus-Cortina, and BMW, with its 1800TiSA – could do, Alfa decided to go one better. Like the rivals, there would be two major improvements, both made with an eye to improving the power/weight ratio: raising the horsepower and reducing the weight. A third factor, which the opposition had also employed – improving the roadholding – was not necessary, as the Giulia GT already had a fine chassis. In this way, the evolution of the new Giulia GTA (A = *Alleggerita* = lightened) got underway.

Technicalities

Although the 1,570cc engine was already a fine and very tuneable twin-cam unit, this was the moment at which Alfa Romeo introduced its new cylinder head casting, which had two sparking plugs per cylinder – one slightly ahead of the cylinder centre line, one slightly behind it. Although this made little or no difference to the performance of the standard road car power unit – which was to be rated at 115bhp at 6,000rpm – it promised even more power when the engine was in full racing tune.

Not every engine tuner, incidentally, agreed that such niceties were helpful; it may be significant that neither Lotus (with the 8-valve twin-cam engine used in the Lotus-Cortina and the Escort Twin-Cam) nor Cosworth (with the 16-valve BDA used in the Escort RS1600) ever used twin ignition.

Alfa's only reaction to this was to point out that full-house 1.6-litre GTAs produced 170bhp at 7,500rpm, which made them fully competitive, and often outright race winners. In any case, removing the plugs from the very centre of the chamber was also done for pragmatic reasons: it eventually allowed the valves to be enlarged, to encourage more fuel-air mixture into and out of the part-spherical combustion chambers.

The remainder of the chassis was much like that of the Giulia Sprint GT/GTV, with the same basic five-speed gearbox, final drive ratio, four-wheel disc brakes and suspension layout. With the GTA, however, for competition purposes there was to be a wide choice of internal gearbox *and* final drive ratios.

The biggest challenge was to get the weight down. The Giulia Sprint GT weighed 2,095lb (950kg), which simply could not compete with the 1,820lb (825kg) of the Lotus-Cortina (and the 'works' cars tended to race in even lighter condition). Accordingly, Alfa Romeo arranged for the GTA to be skinned almost entirely in aluminium instead of steel panels, the only exception being the sills, which were structural and could not be lightened. At the same time, everything possible was stripped out of the cabin – the interior was spartan, to say the least – while

magnesium alloy castings replaced aluminium for clutch bell-housing, rear gearbox plate, front engine cover, and camshaft covers.

Except for the presence of the famous quadrifoglio (four-leaf clover) badge on the flanks of the shell, there were no visual differences between GTA and GT which, in road car guise, still had front and rear bumpers, though these were often discarded for motor racing – always, where the regulations allowed.

The result, first shown to the public at the Amsterdam Motor Show of January 1965, was a much lighter car than before. How much lighter was often open to discussion. Alfa Romeo claimed that the saving was 452lb (205kg) – which would certainly make the car competitive in saloon car racing – though its original press information was that the saving was 200lb (90kg). Other histories have claimed a weight reduction of 710lb (322kg), which is quite impossible to justify.

Race cars were, of course, lighter still, for Group 2 regulations allowed bumpers to be removed and perspex to replace glass in the side and rear windows, while magnesium Campagnolo wheels with lightweight racing tyres were always specified.

Career

Although the 1.6-litre GTA was exhibited again at the Geneva Motor Show in March 1965, sales and deliveries took time to build up. Like their rivals (Ford and BMC were both amazingly adept at this, too), sporting homologation was achieved a long time before the necessary 1,000 cars had been produced. In August 1963, when approval came, I doubt if the company had delivered more than the first 200 examples! In fact, Alfa Romeo's own publication *Tutte le Vetture dal 1910* ('*All Cars from 1910*') tells us that only 406 GTAs were assembled in 1965, only 21 in 1966, and 61 in 1967, followed by 12 in 1969 (all of which were turned into GTAm types by Autodelta). All in all, exactly 500 1.6-litre GTAs, of which 50 had right-hand steering, were built in five years – a respectable number, but strictly enough to satisfy the authorities (if they had known . . .).

So, what if the necessary 1,000 cars were not sold? The fact is that Alfa Romeo was ready and willing to build as many such cars as could be sold, but the marketplace for fragile, lightweight, no-compromise racing 'saloons' like this was strictly limited, as Ford soon discovered when it marketed the Escort Twin-Cam.

In motorsport, GTAs prepared and campaigned by Autodelta did exactly what had been hoped. First seen in prototype form in 1965, they showed promise. The first head-to-head battles with Sir John Whitmore's Lotus-Cortina came at the end of the year – at Snetterton, after 500km, Whitmore won, while Bussinello's GTA (having led for the first two hours) took second place: the marker had been laid down.

In 1966 Autodelta ran a team throughout the year, with the young F1 star Jochen Rindt drafted in to bolster the line-up. Once again, in the European Touring Car (ETC) Championship the battle was mainly with Sir John Whitmore's Alan Mann Racing Lotus-Cortina – and this time the Alfa was on top, winning all but a handful of events.

Twitchy enough on the road, on the race track the GTA was a great car to drive, but looked frightening from trackside. To get the power on to the ground at all times, Autodelta developed the chassis with a soft rear end (which ensured that the inside rear wheel was usually 'on the deck') and with stiff front suspension. This meant that a hard-driven GTA could often be seen three-wheeling its way through the bends, the inside front wheel well in the air! And sometimes, if the limited-slip differential was wound up tight enough, and if super-grip racing rubber was fitted, the inside rear wheel would lift as well.

Thereafter, the GTA had even more formidable opposition. From 1967 Porsche joined in (though Alfa won the European Touring Car series once again), having convinced the CSI that the 911 was a 'saloon car', and from 1968 there was the Escort Twin-Cam. But the GTA could still win the ETC, which it did, and before it was retired the 1.6-litre GTA (driven by Spartaco Dini) once again won the 1,600cc division of the ETC.

In the meantime, the original GTA had spawned three more developments – the GTA 1300 Junior, which was a genuine production car, and the GTAms, which were not.

GTA 1300 Junior

Alfa Romeo was, above all, a pragmatic concern and, as we have seen, was adept at filling in tiny corners of its range of cars. Realizing that the Porsche 911 was likely to outrun the 1.6-litre GTAs, it decided to build faster and more specialized GTAs (the GTAms: *see* page 113), and also to produce a smaller-engined version of the car, to be known as the GTA 1300 Junior.

In marketing terms, this made a great deal of sense, for the mainstream GT 1300 Junior had gone on sale in 1966, and there was always a demand, in Italy and elsewhere, for cars to race in the thriving 1.3-litre class. Here, then, was a chance to get a 1.3-litre 'saloon car' homologated – and for it to replace the white-hot racing Giulietta saloons which were showing their age.

The GTA 1300 Junior was launched in June 1968, and was exactly what the enthusiasts had hoped for. Structurally and in its styling, 'little brother' was exactly like the 1.6-litre GTA (which was nearing the end of its life), complete with a body shell mostly in aluminium panels, and with a simply trimmed interior: at 1,676lb (760kg) it weighed almost the same as the 1.6-litre car. This time, though, the engine was a unique 96bhp/1,290cc version of the famous twin-cam, complete with the twin-spark-plug cylinder head; in standard form not as powerful as the Giulietta SS/SZ types had been, but with more potential for race tuning.

Nor was this an ordinary 1.3-litre. This time it was nothing less than a short-stroke version of the 1.6-litre GTA unit, with a 78mm cylinder bore, which meant that the original 1.6-litre twin-plug head could be used without modification, and that it was potentially an even higher revving engine than usual. For comparison:

Original 1.3-litre Giulietta	1,290cc, 74mm bore × 75mm stroke
GTA 1300	1,290cc 78mm bore × 67.5mm stroke

Same basis, but two very different variations on the theme. On the left, complete with four headlamps, is one of the formidable 2000 GTAms of 1971 (note the later-type front-end sheet-metal styling), whose race-tune engine produced up to 240bhp. On the right is a GTA 1300 Junior, complete with 160bhp/1.3-litre racing engine and the original 'step-front' style.

The GTA 1300 Junior was just that: a 'junior', or smaller, version of the already successful Giulia GTA, still with the lightweight bodywork and all the mechanical options, but this time with a 1,290cc engine that produced 96bhp in standard tune. There were 447 such cars built from 1968 to 1972.

This very special engine was in fact the only oversquare derivative of the twin-cam ever sold to the general public.

Using twin dual-choke Weber carburettors, Autodelta eventually liberated 160bhp at 8,300rpm from this magnificent car – equal to the power output of 1.6-litre Alfas of only three or four years earlier – and then made it available with Alfa-SPICA fuel-injection, when it produced 165bhp at 8,400rpm.

Once again, here was a car that struggled to sell, and although it was eventually homologated as a Group 2 machine (which means that Alfa Romeo claimed that 1,000 such cars had been built), Alfa records show that just 447 were produced from 1968 to 1972: 320 in 1968, 82 in 1969, 8 in 1970, 22 in 1971 and just 15 in 1972. To quote that eminent Alfa enthusiast Phil Llewellin: 'the response to this [homologation] requirement included the wondrously

simple trick of skipping chassis numbers. According to those who have investigated the subject, finding two cars with consecutive numbers is only a tad easier than meeting a unicorn while strolling down London's Oxford Street'.

This was a racing-car-for-the-road which delivered on both counts. In standard form – few cars ever remained like this – it could approach 109mph (175kph), but in full race tune it was good for 130mph (209kph), when the engine could be singing along at 8,000rpm and more, and could continue to do so for lengthy endurance races.

Though the factory was not interested in campaigning the GTA 1300 Junior (they were in a different league with the Tipo 33 racing sports car by then), it soon proved to be an excellent private-owner's 'class car' and would be used all round Europe until the early 1970s.

The GTA 1300 Junior looked ready to race, even when standing still, though many such cars were lowered considerably for circuit events. Like the Giulia GTA, it was supplied without front or rear bumpers.

GTA-SA

Although this supercharged version of the GTA was purely a racing car, and only ten were ever built by Autodelta in 1967 and 1968, it was technically interesting. Produced specifically for Group 5 touring car racing (this was virtually an 'anything goes' formula, though a car's standard body shell and engine block had to be retained), the SA (*Sovralimentata* = Supercharged) used a very special derivative of the GTA engine, which produced 220bhp at 7,500rpm.

Once again, there had been a reshuffle of the bore and stroke dimensions, for these differed from those of the normal GTA:

GTA   1,570cc, 78mm bore × 82mm stroke
GTA-SA   1,568cc, 86mm bore × 67.5mm stroke

The cylinder bore, therefore, was the largest ever used in this engine, the stroke being that of the GTA 1300 Junior. This may have done nothing for the engine's low-speed torque, but it was yet another high-revving Alfa twin-cam that did a great job on the circuits. Interestingly enough, Alfa usually quoted the engine capacity as '1,570cc', if only to suggest to the public that it was a lightly-modified GTA power unit.

By any standards this was a complex power unit, for the twin dual-choke Weber carburettors were fed by twin centrifugal superchargers (not turbos), which were driven from the engine by chain-driven hydraulic pumps, the pressurized fuel-air mixture also being treated to water-injection (for intercooling purposes) as it entered the combustion chambers. Not the sort of engine that could sensibly be put into production, even on a limited scale.

This, in fact, was a short-lived car for short-distance races, and had only limited success, though there were race wins in France and Germany, and class victories around Europe.

1750 GTAm and 2000 GTAm – For Racing Only

The GTAms, of which only forty were produced, all by Autodelta, in 1970 and 1971, were pure racing saloons. So do they qualify for study in this book? In that they were lineal developments of the original GTAs (though much heavier), in homologation terms indeed they do, though once again these were further developments of the Giulia Sprint GT/GTA theme.

The 'Am' name, incidentally, refers to the American market, for by this time the series-production Sprint GT had become the 1750 GT Veloce (later the 2000 GT Veloce) and was being strongly marketed in the USA. The very same fleet of cars were called 1750 GTAm in 1970, and 2000 GTAm in 1971.

Produced especially for Group 2 European Touring Car Championship 'saloon' car racing, the GTAms pushed the letter (and spirit!) of the regulations to the absolute limit, though because the GTA had never been made with an engine larger than 1.6 litres, that car's light-alloy-skinned structure could not be used.

The basis of these cars, therefore, was the all-steel hull of the 1750 GTV/2000 GTV coupés, which unfortunately meant that they would be considerably heavier than the GTAs had ever been – 2,029lb (920kg) instead of 1,643lb (745kg) – though regulations allowed them to run with magnificently flared front and rear wheelarches to hide the fat, 9in-wide, 13in racing rubber on which they ran.

Using all the well-known GTA chassis tweaks, along with a colossal choice of transmission and final drive ratios, both types of Ams – 1750 in 1970 and 2000 in 1971 – were powered by 1,985cc twin-cam engines, these being an amalgam of twin-spark GTA top end, 2000 GTV bottom end, and a slight overbore – 84.5mm instead of 84mm – from the 2000 GTV's standard size. Fuel supply was by SPICA fuel-injection, the valves were enlarged yet again, and the compression ratio boosted to 11.0:1. In 1970 form, the quoted power output was as high as 220bhp at 7,200rpm (that long stroke set limits to the revolutions which could be achieved), while for the second season, engines could produce up to 240bhp at 7,500rpm. This was quite remarkable for a long-stroke 8-valve power output. At the time, Ford would not have found it easy to beat this with their own 16-valve BDA units in the Escort RS1600 race cars.

Alfa reliability tied to a racing top speed of up to 149mph (240kph) meant that the 1750 GTAm/2000 GTAm types were formidable competitors. In the 1970 European Touring Car Championship, Toine Hezemans easily won the Championship (and the large-car Division 3) outright, with Gian-Luigi Picchi's sister car second, there being five Ams in the top ten. Hezemans won four races outright – including the prestige race at Monza – and was class of the field in a season in which a GTA 1300 Junior won Division 1 (for 1.6-litre cars).

In 1971 it was a slightly different story, for the categories had been changed, and the GTAm found itself in Division 2, for 2-litre cars, while Ford's colossally powerful (290bhp) Capri RS2600s had been homologated in Division 3. Even so, Alfa Romeo figured strongly in the Manufacturers' series, tying for outright victory, while Toine Hezemans was once again dominant in his division, winning five of the eight races.

GT1300 Junior Zagato and 1600 Junior Zagato

By 1969 the Giulia range was well established, and had already been on the market for seven years. It was a year in which no fewer than nine different derivatives (plus a trio of updated '1750s') were fighting each other for space on the assembly lines at Arese.

The GT 1300 Junior Z, with styling and body construction by Zagato, was one of the most appealing of all derivatives on this versatile platform. As far as shapes were concerned, Zagato had good days and bad days – this one had been a brilliant day.

Time, then, for Alfa Romeo to take a rest, perhaps? Yet this was a year in which a brand new Giulia-based shape came along (the first new sporty shape on this platform since the arrival of the 1600 Spider in 1966): the GT 1300 Junior Zagato. This beautiful little coupé's title tells most of the story, for clearly it was based on the existing platform of the Giulia GT 1300 Junior and the 1750 Spider, but it boasted a style by Zagato. All production cars, incidentally, had left-hand steering.

It was the style itself that made all the difference. Although Zagato was not one of Alfa Romeo's regular or favoured coachbuilders (in recent years it had only produced the Giulietta SZ and the shells for the Tubolare Zagato), it was a respected local concern.

The new car was unveiled, in prototype form, at the Turin Motor Show of November 1969, and caused a real stir. Demonstrably intended for road use, though based on the ultra-short 88.6in (2,250mm) wheelbase platform of the existing Spider, it was a sexy little two-seater fastback coupé, quite unlike any other car in Alfa's range.

Zagato not only tackled the styling (which was, in some ways, an artistic relative of the Lancia Fulvia Zagatos for which the company was also responsible), but also provided all the body shells for the production cars. These would be in conventional steel rather than the wafer-thin aluminium panelling that Zagato had previously supplied for earlier sporting Alfas.

The two-seater style was at once unique and practical, distinctly wedge-nosed in profile, wide and flat across the bonnet, and with more glass area than any previous Giulia-based coupé. In the

The GT 1300 Junior Z looked good from every possible angle, even under the potentially flat lighting of a vast motor show stand. It was only a two-seater, naturally.

Zagato built the 1.3-litre-engined GT 1300 Junior Z from 1969 to 1972, then followed it up with the 1.6-litre 1600 Junior Z from 1972 to 1975. The body style was peerless, and never needed retouching or improvement.

This was the facia/instrument panel layout of the Junior Z, as revealed in 1969, with the gear lever protruding out of the centre console in that typical Alfa Romeo manner.

nose there were four circular headlamps, covered by perspex shrouds, so cooling air for the engine water radiator had to enter through the centre, where the Alfa shield was more 'black hole' than decoration. The front bumpers were really an apology for such, as they were extremely small and thin in section.

Typically for Zagato, the bonnet line, sleek until shortly in front of the screen, suddenly flipped up to hide the wiper arms and blades. Behind the line of the front seats, the line of the roof swept smoothly down over the near-horizontal rear window, which really qualified as a 'glassback'. As with the Fulvia Z coupé which Zagato also produced, the rear window was hinged at its front end, and could be opened by a couple of inches using electric motor screw actuation.

Because it only had an 89bhp/1,290cc engine – identical to that used in the 'mainstream' sporty 1300s – and the whole car weighed a sturdy 2,029lb (920kg), this pretty little Zagato-inspired machine looked faster than it was. Although it had a claimed top speed of 109mph (175kph), Alfa enthusiasts had to take this on trust, for no independent road tests seem to have been published.

There were three major reasons why this individual-looking Alfa coupé did not sell faster than it did. One was certainly that there was a limit to how many body shells Zagato could actually supply; another was that deliveries did not actually begin until 1970; or perhaps it was the relatively high selling price – 2,235,000 lira in 1970, compared with just 1,665,000 lira for the GT 1300 Junior, a hike of 34 per cent – which limited its otherwise considerable appeal.

Whatever the reason, between its launch in 1969, and late 1972, only 1,108 such cars were ever produced – 566 in 1970, 358 in 1971 and 184 in 1972 – after which it was replaced.

The later derivative, which was introduced at the end of 1972, was a relatively simple upgrade, by the fitment of a 1.6-litre engine. Thus, the 1600 Junior Zagato model was born, complete with the 109bhp/1,570cc engine previously seen in the Giulia Sprint GTV. Visual and equipment

changes were limited to the use of more sturdy front and rear bumpers and larger rear light clusters, though Zagato had no need to alter the styling at all. With 109bhp, the claimed top speed rose to 118mph (190kph), though at the same time the price rose to 2,620,000 lira.

But here was another sporty Alfa that did not commercially live up to its promise. In three years only 402 such cars were produced, and the line was finally dropped in 1975.

Giulia Coupé Family – Production Figures

1,290cc	
GT 1300 Junior	91,964
GTA 1300 Junior	492
GT 1300 Junior Z	1,108

1,570cc	
Sprint GT	21,850
Sprint GT Veloce	12,499
GTA 1600	493
1600 Junior Z	402
TZ1/TZ2 (Zagato)	124

1,779cc	
1750GTV	44,276

1,962cc	
2000 GTV	37,921

| Total | 211,129 |

Montreal – V8-Engined Supercar

The most extreme of all the Giulia Sprint GT-derived coupés was held over until 1970, was mechanically the most changed, and qualified as a Supercar in almost every way. This was the famous V8-engined Montreal, which was in production from 1971 to 1977.

Public opinion can make a lot of difference. What was originally intended only as a show car, or at best a limited-production machine, and seen at Expo '67 in Montreal, Canada, created such a stir at that exhibition that it was developed, made

The Montreal started its public career as a show car at Expo '67 in Montreal. This was the original show car, the only major style difference with later road cars being the front end.

If you think the Montreal road car looks exactly the same as that of the Expo '67 show car think again. Compare the two cars and you will see a different front-end, wheelarch flares on the production car, different wheels, different door pillar/front wing details, six cooling slats instead of seven and a repositioned filler cap.

easier to build in larger quantities, and was put on sale within three years.

The 'Montreal' project began in the winter of 1966–67, when the organizers of the forthcoming Expo '67 World Fair invited Alfa and Bertone 'to exhibit a car which satisfies the highest attainable ideals of man in the field of auto engineering'.

Initial information about the show cars (two were built for exhibition in Canada), which were unveiled in April 1967, was sparse, for Alfa originally talked about producing between 50 and 100 cars, though they cautiously agreed that this might be increased to 500 cars if there was sufficient demand. At the same time it was hinted, but never confirmed, that the new body covered a version of the mid-V8-engined Tipo 33 racing sports car that Alfa had just unveiled. The existence of stylized air intakes behind the doors (close, in other words, to the mythical location of a mid-mounted engine), and a lack of confirmation from anyone at Alfa Romeo, made this sound deliciously possible.

Yet it was all hearsay, for Alfa had never considered making such a car, and in March 1970, when the Montreal production car appeared at the Geneva Motor Show, it became clear that the Expo '67 show cars had been produced on the platform of the Giulia Sprint GTV. Stories persist, in fact, that they did not actually have engines fitted at that moment!

The Montreal, based on a 1967 show car, was launched in 1970 and built until 1977, all cars having this same semi-hooded headlamp front-end treatment.

The production car, though considerably different in detail from the 1967 show cars, was a deliciously-styled two-seater coupé, with rounded lines, a long, sloping 'glassback' tail, all powered by a detuned version of the modern Alfa Romeo racing V8 engine. With 200bhp from 2.6 litres, this was by far the most powerful road car version ever to use the Type 105 Giulia platform which had first appeared in 1962.

Style Changes

Bertone of Turin, always one of Alfa Romeo's favourite contractors, got the job of building as many Montreal shells as the market would accept. As with the current 1750 GTV project, Alfa Romeo provided platforms and Bertone completed the sheet metal, before the nearly complete structure was transported back to Milan.

In detail, if not in concept or general proportions, there were many differences between the show cars and the Montreal that went into production (*see* page 118). Most obvious were the different front-end treatment, the wheel-arch flares, the wheels themselves, a new filler cap cover, six intake slats instead of seven, and most significantly a different style of integrated windscreen/A-post pillars, doors and front wings.

The basic proportions remained, for, along with sexy slatted covers over the upper crescent of the four headlamps, and with a central NASA-style air intake duct in the bonnet panel, this always looked like a seriously purposeful machine. The 195-section tyres and the many-spoked light-alloy wheels all helped.

Although the platform itself, along with the suspension and steering layout, were familiar enough, the engine and transmission were new. The engine was a detuned, productionized, derivative of that which Autodelta's Carlo Chiti had inspired in the mid-1960s, and which Alfa had been using in sports car racing from 1967. In racing form, the original 2.0-litre/270bhp engine had already been enlarged to 3.0 litres/440bhp at 9,800rpm, so a road car version of 2.6 litres, with a torquey 200bhp, was not likely to be overstressed.

The Montreal's wet-liner V8 was, in truth, very different from the racing unit in many ways, though the general architecture was unaltered, and along with the existing 1750 GTV, it shared the same classic twin-cam cylinder head layout, the valves being operated by inverted bucket-type tappets. Block and heads were both in light alloy, with steel liners, and fuel supply was by the latest SPICA fuel-injection system.

Because Alfa's existing Giulia-style five-speed gearbox could not deal with the V8 engine's towering 173lb ft of torque, a new box was needed, so Alfa Romeo took the pragmatic choice of buying in supplies of the latest German ZF five-speeder – the same basic gearbox that was already being fitted to cars as diverse as the front-engined Fiat Dino 2400, the rallying versions of the Ford Escort RS1600, and would later be adopted by Vauxhall for the Chevette HS, and by Peugeot-Talbot for the Sunbeam-Lotus.

The rear axle, incidentally, might have looked exactly like that already being used in other cars of the Giulia family, but had been beefed up, internally, as far as possible.

Although the Montreal came to market at the right time – this was pre-energy crisis Europe, after all, while the safety and exhaust emission regulations in the USA (where the Montreal was also to be marketed) were not as restricting as they would become in mid-decade – it was never going to be easy to break into a sector dominated by Ferrari and Maserati. Alfa Romeo realized this, and set the original price tag at 5,200,000 lira, which was more than twice that of the 1750 GTV (which sold for 2,495,000 lira), but significantly cheaper than the Ferrari Dino of the day.

Although Alfa Romeo was rightly proud of what had been achieved, neatly and with great style, on this familiar platform, the fact was that the Montreal was really only halfway to being an outstanding car. In a world in which Ferraris tended to have much larger engines and more than 300bhp, and where 2.4-litre Porsches were just as fast yet cheaper, there would be a struggle. Even so, the Montreal could achieve 137mph (220kph), with a 0–60mph sprint in 7.6 seconds, and like all other Italian cars of its type it made the most exciting engine noises along the way.

As with many such limited-production Italian cars, it is not easy to arrive at precise production statistics. Alfa Romeo state that the Montreal was on sale from 1970 to 1977, yet deliveries do not seem to have begun until the first weeks of 1971, and the last cars were apparently completed in 1976. On the other hand, the number of Montreals actually built is not in doubt – 3,925, including a limited number of right-hand-drive examples from 1974. About 700 cars were built in the first season (1971), and the car's prospects looked good. Until, that is, word of V8 engine unreliability began to spread and, from late 1973, the market-depressing effects of the energy crisis took effect.

By 1975 the Montreal had been virtually forgotten and was allowed to die, without ceremony, before the end of 1976. Alfa Romeo never noted its passing, and certainly did not contemplate replacing it.

6 Alfetta GT – A Bold New Layout

Alfa Romeo enthusiasts greeted the launch of the technically interesting Alfetta saloon of 1972 with great interest. As far as the range of saloons was concerned, its arrival was not a moment too soon, for Alfa's mainstream customers were getting bored with what was on offer. It wasn't that Alfa Romeo had allowed its range to stagnate, but that its precarious financial position meant that it had been obliged to mix-and-match from a limited list of ingredients for a lengthy period. Since 1962, the number of Giulia derivatives had grown and grown, for even the 1750/2000 were evolutions of the same platform.

The sporting cars, at least, were somewhat fresher, but even there, the only recent technical novelty had been the arrival of the V8-engined Montreal, which was expensive, and even the platform of that car was Giulia-based. Nothing truly novel, therefore, had been seen since 1963.

By 1972, in fact, the Giulia Sprint GT family had been on sale for nine years, in four engine sizes and any number of different titles and equipment packages. The open-topped Spider, having grown to its full 2-litre size, was all set for a long run.

Another problem was that, apart from the race-derived V8 of the Montreal, Alfa Romeo coupé and Spider customers hadn't seen a new engine for a long time. By this time, let us not forget, the classic little four-cylinder twin-cam had already been in full production for seventeen years.

New Thinking

The technical staff at Arese had not been idle, however. With the Giulia/1750/2000 generation of saloon already on its way to a tenth birthday, they were finally unleashed on a new family of cars. Although they would be required to use updated derivatives of the existing, and rightly-

Famous name, entirely different type of car. From 1938 to 1951, the Alfetta was one of the world's most successful racing cars, and quite dominant in Grand Prix racing from 1946 to 1951. This was the Tipo 158, and complete with front-mounted engine and rear gearbox/final drive assembly, it gave its name to a 1970s generation of Alfa road cars.

Not the most startling of styles, but the Alfetta saloon was a long-running model which sold well and later donated its platform/underpinnings to cars like the new-generation Giulietta, the 75 and the 90 types.

famous, 'small' twin-cam engine, they were given a free hand.

As ever, the new-generation car would start life as a four-door saloon, and Alfa then planned to spawn off sporting derivatives. In the beginning it was hoped that there would be coupé and spider versions of the new car, but although studies were made and show cars exhibited, no open-top version would ever go on sale.

Work on the new series of cars, which would carry the chassis number prefix '116', got under-way in the late 1960s, the intention being to develop an altogether more modern car than the 2000 saloon, even if it was to be a very similar size overall. Because a previous larger Alfa — the unsuccessful 2600 — had been dropped in 1969, in the fullness of time the new machine would have to become the company flagship, too, as the 2000 could not be expected to have a long life.

It would, on the other hand, be carefully pack-aged to be a very similar size to the Giulia-derived 2000, with which it would run concur-rently, for it would have to be significantly smaller than the 2600 had ever been. One significant rea-son for choosing this package was that the Ital-ians seemed to be averse to buying large cars — domestic ones, at least. Alfa, Fiat and Lancia all found it difficult to sell 'large' cars, where import-ed machinery from Mercedes-Benz and BMW held a majority share of that market.

The obsolete 2600 had in fact been a com-mercial failure — from 1962 to 1969, only 2,038 of these six-cylinder-engined saloons had been sold, and of those a mere 133 had been built in the final four years. There was no enthusiasm, therefore, for producing a replacement.

This, then, is how the new 116 saloon car series lined up against the current 2000, and against the old 2600:

Dimension	2000 (Giulia-based)	Alfetta	2600
Wheelbase	101.1in (2,567mm)	98.9in (2,512mm)	107.1in (2,720mm)
Overall Length	172.8in (4,389mm)	168.5in (4,279mm)	185.6in (4,714mm)
Width	61.6in (1,564mm)	63.8in (1,620mm)	66.9in (1,699mm)

What was fascinating was that Alfa's engineers had clearly learned a lot about the packaging of modern five-seaters, for although the new car had a slightly enlarged, and wider, cabin than the 2000, it would ride on a wheelbase which was slightly shorter than before.

Right from the start the design team began to home in on a mechanical layout that, in produc-tion car terms, was unique at the time. Although

In the beginning, the Alfetta was conceived as a four-door five-seater saloon. The Giugiaro-shaped GT which followed used the same platform and running gear.

The new Alfetta chassis included this novel type of independent front suspension, complete with longitudinal torsion bars, a separate drag link tying the upper wishbone to the front end of the body shell, and a stout anti-roll bar.

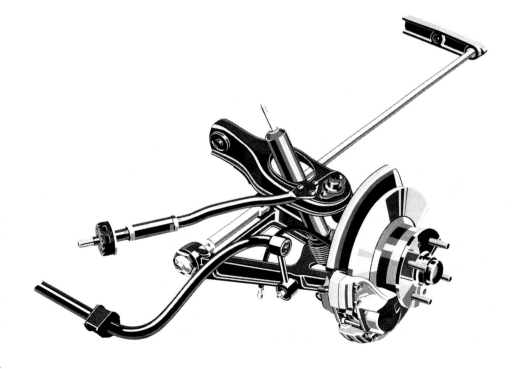

Front Engine, Rear Gearbox – the Correct Solution?

Theoretically, there were good reasons for positioning the gearbox of a front-engined car in the rear, and mounting it in a unit with the final drive ratio, the most compelling being that it moved a heavy lump of metal towards the rear (where it would aid traction), and it allowed a flatter/more spacious front footwell to be provided. Such a layout had already appeared on the Tipo 158 Alfetta single-seater race cars of 1938, which had dominated Grand Prix racing from 1946 to 1951.

However, when Alfa Romeo was evolving the Alfetta, it also discovered the problems – notably those of controlling the antics of an exposed two-piece propeller shaft which was always rotating at engine speed, and of providing a robust clutch to look after this extra inertia.

Once again, Alfa Romeo was technically brave, but when Porsche followed suit with the 924 of 1975, the Germans made several noticeable changes. One was that the clutch reverted to its traditional position (immediately behind the engine), and the other was that they incorporated a massive light-alloy torque tube that connected the (front) engine with the (rear) gearbox, which enclosed a tiny 0.78in diameter propeller shaft supported at four anti-nodal points.

In the years that followed, Alfa Romeo must surely have studied the 924/944 layout to see if it was worth redesigning the Alfetta: they never did.

the engine would stay up front, in the traditional place, its transmission would be located under the rear seats and in unit with the final drive casing. Because this general layout (though not its detailing) was so close to that which had once been used in a previous Alfa Romeo race car – the Tipo 158/159 Alfetta, an all-conquering single-seater Grand Prix car of the 1945–51 period – that generic name was also chosen for the new model.

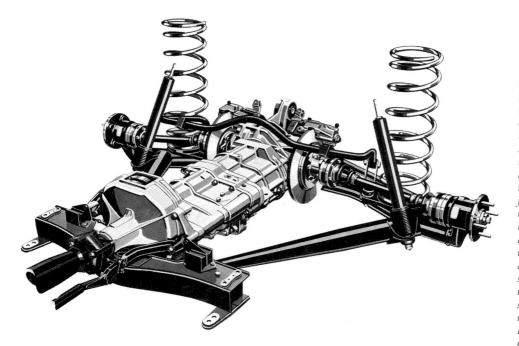

Neat, nicely integrated, but undoubtedly expensive to build, this was the Alfetta's transaxle, rear suspension and rear braking installation. The five-speed gearbox was in unit with the final drive assembly, the clutch was ahead of that, and the rear suspension was by the De Dion system. Not clearly visible here is the De Dion cross-member which linked both wheel hubs together.

But why a new package, especially when the investment involved in tooling up and manufacturing a new rear-mounted transaxle was likely to be very high? It was an installation which, apparently, evolved rather than appeared in a flash on some designer's drawing board. First of all, Alfa Romeo wanted to give its new cars an even better ride/handling/traction balance than they had ever before achieved. To do this, not only was it necesssary to get rid of the age-old rear axle beam, but it would also help if some of the car's unavoidable unsprung weight could be moved towards the rear of the car, and therefore add its effect over the rear wheels.

Getting rid of the rear axle beam left Alfa with two choices – to use all-independent rear suspension, or to use the halfway house of a De Dion system. At this point, another aspiration made the decision easier: the chassis engineers' desire to see that the rear wheels kept vertical, throughout their bump and rebound movement, at all times. This, at a stroke, eliminated simpler cost-attractive independent layouts like those used by BMW, Mercedes-Benz and Triumph – and in came the De Dion, currently used only by Rover.

Modern Platform

Here, then, was the genesis of a new chassis/platform layout, which was brand new for the Alfet-ta, but that would later be adopted for three other new-generation saloons – the reborn late-1970s Giulietta, the 75 model that would eventually replace it, and the 90 range that would eventually take over from the Alfetta.

I am taking pains to analyze the detail of the new layout, even in original saloon car guise, because it had a vital and definite effect on how a future Coupé would operate and look. In packaging terms, one advantage of moving the clutch/gearbox assembly backwards in space – from being in unit with the engine to being in unit with the chassis-mounted differential – meant that it would reduce the unavoidable floorpan bulging on the toeboard, allowing the front passenger footwells to be both wider and, towards the centre of the car, flatter, too. The newly adopted position for the transmission meant that it was effectively in the 'dead' area under the rear seats; this was years before it became fashionable to position the fuel tanks in that part of the car.

Although the range of twin-cam engines was virtually the same as before – the first car to be launched had the 1,779cc size, but it was widely (and correctly) expected that the 1,570cc and 1,962cc sizes would follow – everything else in the drive line was new.

Working backwards down the drive line, a two-piece open propeller shaft linked the engine to an integrated and rear-mounted assembly

---

De Dion

In motoring terms, it seems, nothing is new. Although the use of De Dion rear suspension made sense for Alfa Romeo in the 1970s, such a suspension had first been seen in a car designed by Comte Albert de Dion before the end of the nineteenth century. Then, as later, the object was to reduce unsprung weight by separating the heavy rear axle casing from the wheels themselves, while connecting those wheels by a metal bar or tube to keep them upright at all times.

Abandoned in the early twentieth century, De Dion again made the headlines when adopted by Mercedes-Benz for its phenomenal W125 GP cars. It worked so well that other racing marques rushed to copy. Alfa Romeo adopted De Dion in 1940 for its (unraced) Tipo 512 race car, but did not add it to another model until 1951, for the final derivation of the famous Tipo 159 model.

In the 1950s and 1960s, a De Dion layout was successfully used by Lancia in the Aurelia model, and by Rover in the 2000/3500 range, but it was never fully accepted by mass-production manufacturers.

A De Dion rear suspension featured in every Alfetta-derived car until the last of the Zagato-built RZ models was produced in 1993.

comprising the clutch, a five-speed gearbox, and the final drive unit. (This entire assembly, incidentally, was also integrated to the rear suspension layout and the inboard rear disc brakes, in what was a very elegantly detailed installation.)

To keep its bulk to an absolute minimum, the all-indirect five-speed transmission was laid out 'flat' – the layshaft, in other words, was to the left of the mainshaft, rather than below it in a conventional front-positioned design – its main casing being bolted up direct to the final drive housing.

The propeller shaft, though sturdy, was very carefully mounted to minimize any chance of what is known as a 'whirling' vibration setting in at high speeds. At the front it was connected to the engine through a rubber 'doughnut' joint, and its central steady bearing was supported on the same cross-member that absorbed front suspension loads. The rear shaft – which connected the steady bearing to the transmission – had a rubber doughnut joint at each end.

With the gearchange lever positioned between the seats, four feet or more ahead of the transmission casing itself, it was going to be a real challenge to provide accurate gear selection, and Alfa tried to do this by providing a sturdy in-box linkage, and a straightforward linkage up the centre of the car, alongside the propeller shaft.

Chassis Innovations

All this was matched by a new suspension, braking and steering package, which promised much for the future. All were entirely novel, there being no carryover parts (or even carryover thinking) from previous Alfas.

Structurally, the key to this lay in the design of the floorpan, where the main beam and torsional strength of the body shell was located. In order to keep most of the suspension stresses concentrated in the centre of that floorpan, the engineers arranged for some front suspension loads to be fed back towards cross-members in that strong point, and for some rear suspension loads to be taken forward. Those beams, in fact, were close

together – one ahead of and one just behind the front seat location.

At the front of the car, the geometry of what was a double wishbone looked straightforward enough, though in detail it was not. The upper 'wishbone' was effectively a pressed transverse link tied up to a forward-facing drag link. The bottom wishbone itself was a wide-based pressing, but springing was provided by long torsion bars leading back from the inner pivots of that bottom wishbone to mountings on a transverse body-shell beam positioned just ahead of the front-seat position. The telescopic damper was symmetrically mounted in line with the front hub, inclined inwards, and poking out neatly through a hole in the upper transverse link.

In many ways this layout was a tribute to Jaguar's long-running system, first seen in the XK120 of 1948, and later uprated for use in the famous E-Type sports car. Not only did it provide a very elegant package, but by altering the settings at the rear of the torsion bars, the ride height could be adjusted very simply.

Naturally there was a stout anti-roll bar linking the bottom wishbones, and this was the first full-sized Alfa Romeo to be given rack-and-pinion steering (though a similar system had already been previewed in the small, new-generation, front-wheel-drive Alfasud: *see* Chapter 7).

Viewed from above, the basic geometry of the De Dion rear suspension was a triangle, with the fabricated De Dion tube forming a rigid link between the rear wheel hubs, the tube itself being located sideways by a Watts linkage aft of the tube.

Fore and aft location was by two semi-trailing, tapering tubular arms, fixed to the rear hubs, and at their front ends pivoting from the massive pressed and welded structural cross-member that also formed the front support for the clutch/gearbox/final drive assembly. Vast coil springs were placed at each side, above the De Dion tube, with telescopic dampers mounted ahead of them, and bearing on brackets close to the junction of the De Dion tube and the semi-trailing arms.

Disc brakes all round – at the front in the conventional position close to the front wheel hubs, but at the rear mounted on the inboard flanges of the drive shafts (and therefore very close to the final drive casing) – completed a novel and forward-looking layout.

By comparison, the style of the new car was distinctly ordinary, perhaps predictably so, for Alfa Romeo's family cars had rarely looked as attractive as the sporty versions that grew out of them. This four-door five-seater had been conceived at a time when no stylist and very few engineers thought twice about aerodynamic efficiency (petrol was still cheap and plentiful, but all that was about to change), so the front-end detailing was distinctly conventional, and the drag coefficient (Cd) was reputedly 0.42.

Although Alfa Romeo was, by this time, co-operating with a number of distinguished Italian styling houses – Bertone, Pininfarina and Zagato were already providing body shells for sporting models – none of these companies was brought in to help shape the Alfetta saloon, which was strictly an in-house production.

Alfetta – GT Follows Saloon

By the time the world's press were introduced to the Alfetta in Trieste in May 1972, it was already in full production at Arese, the claim being that 100 cars a week were being assembled, and that this would be increased to 600 per week in due course. Plans were already being laid for a 1.6-litre version to be launched (May 1976), and a 2-litre version (originally for sale only in fuel-injected form in the USA) followed at the same time.

Alfa-watchers recognized the pattern – if the saloon was on the market, could faster and more sporty versions be far behind? – but they had to wait until 1974. Perhaps the gracious Alfetta coupé might have appeared a little earlier had it not been for the onset of an important worldwide economic cataclysm: the Suez War of October 1973, and the shortage of crude oil (the energy crisis) which followed it almost at once. Some companies – notably Fiat – panicked for a time

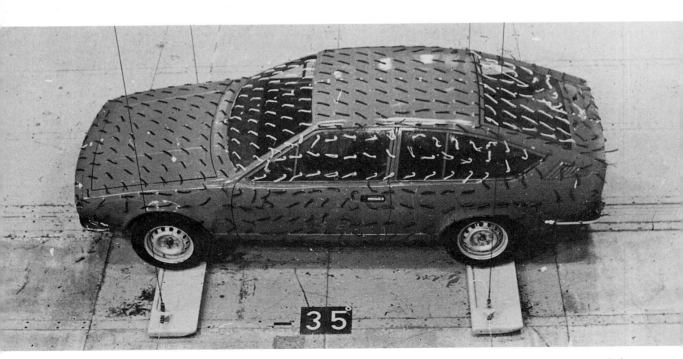

Although Alfa Romeo claimed that the shape of their new Alfetta GT had been refined in the wind tunnel, few changes were made from the style proposed by Giorgetto Giugiaro.

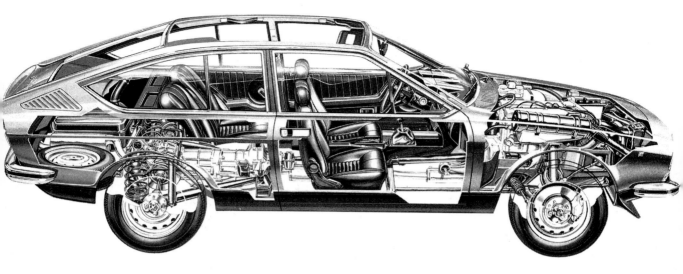

This was the architecture of the original 1.8-litre-engined Alfetta GT of 1974, complete with its torsion bar front suspension, with rear-mounted transaxle and De Dion rear suspension. Styling of the hatchback was by Giugiaro.

Series-production, Alfa Romeo style, at Arese, where the Alfetta GT bodies were welded together in the mid-1970s.

and cancelled various new-model programmes. Alfa Romeo, however, took a cautious line, watched how its rivals were coping and what was happening in the world, and eventually launched a car called the Alfetta GT in May 1974. By this time the Alfetta saloon was already being judged as a success, for no fewer than 65,000 of those cars had already been produced.

The formula for the new coupé was recognizable, but the detail treatment was not. As ever, Alfa

Alfetta GT body monocoques near completion at Arese in the mid-1970s. The parallel line is a mixture of Giulia 2000 GTV and 2000 saloon shells with, on the far right, the Alfetta saloon body assembly tracks.

Although much of the Alfetta GT body assembly was jigged and automated, a good deal of hand work was needed to finish off the assembly before it was painted.

Alfetta GT/GTV/GTV 6 (1974–87, all types)

Layout

Unit-construction body-chassis structure, with steel panels. Two-door, front engine/rear transmission/rear drive, sold as 2+2-seater coupé model.

Engine

Four-cylinder:

Block material	Cast aluminium
Head material	Cast aluminium
Cylinders	4 in-line
Cooling	Water
Main bearings	5
Valves	2 per cylinder, operated by twin-overhead camshafts and inverted bucket-type tappets, driven by chain from crankshaft

Alfetta GT 1.6, 1,570cc: bore and stroke 78 × 82mm; compression ratio 9.0:1; two horizontal twin-choke Weber 40DCOE carburettors, Solex C40 DDH-5 or Dellorto DHLA40 types; 109bhp (DIN) @ 5,600rpm, 105lb ft @ 4,300rpm

Alfetta GT 1.8, 1,779cc: bore and stroke 80 × 88.5mm; compression ratio 9.0:1; two horizontal twin-choke Weber 40DCOE carburettors, Solex C40 DDH-5 or Dellorto DHLA40 types; 122bhp (DIN) @ 5,500rpm, 123lb ft @ 4,400rpm

Alfetta GTV 2000, 1,962cc: bore and stroke 84 × 88.5mm; compression ratio 9.0:1; two horizontal twin-choke Weber 40DCOE carburettors, Solex C40 DDH-5 or Dellorto DHLA40 types, 121bhp (DIN) @ 5,300rpm, 129lb ft @ 4,000rpm
(Note: SPICA fuel-injection on USA-market cars, 112bhp (DIN) @ 5,500rpm)
(From 1980, the engine was rerated at 130bhp (DIN) @ 5,400rpm, 132lb ft @ 4,000rpm)

Turbodelta, 1,962cc: bore and stroke 84 × 88.5mm; compression ratio 7.1:1; two horizontal twin-choke carburettors, Dellorto DHLA40 types, 150bhp (DIN) @ 5,500rpm, 170lb ft @ 3,500rpm

V6 cylinder:

Block material	Cast aluminium
Head material	Cast aluminium
Cylinders	6, in 60-degree V-formation
Cooling	Water
Main bearings	4
Valves	2 per cylinder, operated by single-overhead camshaft, plus pushrod and rocker for exhaust valves, and inverted bucket-type tappets, driven by internally cogged belt from nose of crankshaft

Alfetta GTV 6, 2,492cc: bore and stroke 88 × 68.3mm; compression ratio 9.0:1; Bosch L-Jetronic fuel-injection; 160bhp (DIN) @ 5,600rpm, 157lb ft @ 4,000rpm
(Note: for USA market, 156bhp (DIN) @ 5,500rpm, 152lb ft @ 3,200rpm)

Alfetta GTV 6 3.0, 2,935cc: bore and stroke 93 × 72mm; compression ratio 9.0:1; Bosch L-Jetronic fuel-injection; 174bhp (DIN) @ 5,800rpm, 164lb ft @ 4,300rpm

Alfetta GT/GTV/GTV 6 (1974–87, all types) *continued*

Transmission

Five-speed all-synchromesh manual gearbox, mounted in unit with final drive casing

Clutch Single dry plate (four-cylinder cars); twin dry plate diaphragm (six-cylinder cars); hydraulically operated

Internal Gearbox Ratios

[V6-engined car in brackets]

Top	0.83	[0.78]
4th	1.04	[1.026]
3rd	1.37	[1.345]
2nd	2.00	[1.956]
1st	3.30	[3.500]
Reverse	2.62	[3.00]
Final drive	4.10:1 (1.8, 2000, Turbodelta, GTV 6); 4.3:1 (1.6)	

Suspension and Steering

Front	Independent, torsion bars, wishbones, anti-roll bar, telescopic dampers
Rear	De Dion axle, by coil springs, semi-trailing radius arms, Watts linkage, telescopic dampers, anti-roll bar
Steering	Rack-and-pinion
Tyres	185/70HR–14in; 195/60HR–15in (GTV 6)
Wheels	Alloy disc, bolt-on
Rim width	5.5in; 6.0in (GTV 6)

Brakes

Type	Disc brakes at front and rear, hydraulically operated
Size	10.3in front discs, 9.85in dia. rear discs

Dimensions

Track	
Front	53.5in (1,360mm)
Rear	53.5in (1,360mm)
Wheelbase	94.5in (2,400mm)
Overall length	165.0in (4,190mm)
Overall width	65.5in (1,664mm)
Overall height	52.4in (1,330mm)
Unladen weight	
Four-cylinder cars	European spec: 2,205lb (1,000kg)–2,381lb (1,080kg) (depending on model); USA spec: 2,712lb (1,230kg)
GTV 6	European spec: 2,668lb (1,210kg); USA spec: 2,844lb (1,290kg)

Romeo had arranged to produce a shortened-wheelbase version of a saloon car platform, had invited a specialist styling house to develop a new shape, had approved of what was offered, then put the new car into production.

The new 1.8-litre twin-cam car – which, logically enough, was to be titled Alfetta GT – saw several changes of approach from Alfa Romeo

Painted Alfetta GT bodies prepare to descend to floor level, where all the running gear is to be inserted. On the floor, in the left foreground, are three Alfetta gearbox/final drive transaxle assemblies.

Almost complete now, the Alfetta GT, with its classic twin-cam four-cylinder engine, nears the end of the assembly line at Arese.

Giorgetto Giugiaro

In the last thirty years of the twentieth century, the names of Giorgetto Giugiaro, and the Ital Design Company which he founded, were among the most famous of all Italian styling houses.

Born south of Turin in 1938, the young Giugiaro's family had always been accomplished painters and musicians, so there was real artistic blood coursing through his veins. Having graduated from Turin's Academy of Fine Arts in 1955, he then joined the newly-formed Fiat styling studio in Turin. Even though he was only twenty-one years old in 1959, his talents were immediately obvious, this being the year in which Nuccio Bertone persuaded Giorgetto to join Bertone as its chief stylist.

In the next few years, at Bertone, he was credited with several landmark designs, including the original Alfa Romeo 2000/2600 Sprint Coupé and Giulia Sprint GT styles.

In 1965 he joined Ghia (also of Turin), his work there including the Maserati Ghibli and the De Tomaso Mangusta models. Then, in 1968, he set up his own company, Ital Design, which was to seal his reputation for ever.

In the 1970s, Ital Design not only developed the Alfetta GT for Alfetta, but also produced cars as different, and as significant, as the Alfasud, the Lotus Esprit, the VW Golf, the Maserati Bora, the BMW M1 and the De Lorean DMC12, the Fiat Uno and the Saab 9000. Still more startling production model styles, and project cars, were to follow, and Ital Design's enterprise was by no means exhausted, even at the end of the century.

tradition. Not only was this the first sporty car to evolve on the Alfetta platform, but it was also the company's first true sporting hatchback (the Montreal, which had no more than a lift-up rear window, only went halfway down that road), and it had been shaped by Giorgetto Giugiaro.

Giugiaro was not unknown to the company. He was, after all, the individual who had shaped the original Giulia Sprint GT for Bertone in the early 1960s, who had consulted with Alfa Romeo on the style of the new Alfasud, and who, by the early 1970s, had become one of the most high-profile industrial designers in Italy.

Shortening the Alfetta's wheelbase – from 98.8in (2,510mm) to 94.5in (2,400mm) – had been straightforward enough for the engineers, for the only technical change this entailed was to shorten the engine's propeller shaft, and the gearbox linkage then reduced the available length of the cabin by several inches. Not that Alfa Romeo minded this at all – their intent was always to see an Alfetta GT as a generously-proportioned 2+2 rather than as a full four-seater, and in any case they could rely on their newly-hired design genius, Giorgetto Giugiaro, to provide a fine package around the new platform.

Although the Alfetta GT's platform/package was only marginally larger than that of the existing Giulia Sprint GT/2000 GTV – the wheelbase was

2.0in (50mm) longer and the all-important rear track wider by 3.3in (84mm) – Giugiaro somehow made the interior of the new car considerably more spacious than before. The extra volume, which added to the appeal of the new style, was mostly located towards the rear of the cabin, where the roof line swept smoothly down over the rear window/hatch to a sharply cut-off tail, and which featured a tiny transverse spoiler.

Although there was considerably more windscreen rake on the new car, which did not help the driver feel totally at home, from a mid-roof position to the tail the roof line was significantly higher than before, which helped turn the Alfetta GT into an 'almost-four-seater'.

By any standards (and Giugiaro was adept at setting many of Europe's standards at this time), the exterior style was stunning, and almost totally different from the rather undistinguished saloon. At the front, there was a delicately detailed four-headlamp nose, where a simplified version of the Alfa Romeo shield was surrounded by a full-width black grille. Across the nose were 'chin spoilers' which helped to separate a radiator cooling blast from that being channeled underneath the car itself. The drag coefficient (Cd) was quoted at 0.39, creditable for this time, but still high by the standards that would be achieved by the motor industry in the 1990s.

The flanks were smooth and needed no adornment, with simple pull-out bright-work door handles breaking up the mass of the doors, and with triangular-shaped cabin air outlets being positioned at the very rear where the roof swept down to meet what we might once have described as the rear wings. One interesting and thoughtful detail was that the large expanse of glass on the rear quarters was split, so that a size-able panel immediately behind the doors could also be wound down to give fresh air to rear seat passengers.

As already noted, there was a big lift-up hatch-back/rear window at the rear (strangely enough, with a single, centrally-placed support strut). This, as expected, was linked to a lift-up parcel shelf that also acted as a modesty-panel to protect the contents of the tail from prying eyes. This was all well and good, but unlike its rivals' arrange-ments, the swivelling parcel shelf could not be removed, nor could that single strut be discon-nected. To emphasize that this car was not meant to be that esoteric modern breed of car called a 'sporting estate', the rear seats were not arranged to fold forward.

The controversy – initiated by several pundits – was in the instrument layout, which looked awkward when the car was newly announced, and got no better with usage. The original left-hand-drive cars (these were, in any event, expect-ed to make up the vast majority of all Alfetta GTs ever to be made) had a facia which featured a central instrument package containing the speedometer, three auxiliary gauges and several important warning-lamp positions. The rev-counter, on the other hand, was placed directly ahead of the driver's eyes (this, in itself, was praise-worthy) in a separate angular pod, the result look-ing almost as if it was an afterthought, which it was not. There was one distinct advantage, in that the facia of right-hand-drive cars only needed the separate instrument pod to be moved across the car without displacing anything else.

Oddly enough, on right-hand-drive cars, the separate pod was arranged to accommodate the speedometer, the rev-counter being banished

This was the Alfetta GT, as originally launched in 1974. Giugiaro's style was flawless, crisp and unmistakable.

The Alfetta GT was styled around the little-modified platform of the Alfetta saloon. Although the cabin gives close-coupled four-seater hatchback accommodation, Giugiaro's style makes the car look smaller than this.

The Alfetta GT, and two views of the same motor car. On the one hand, the nose was crisply detailed, with four headlamps and the characteristic Alfa Romeo shield, while the tail was a smooth, sweeping hatchback shape.

into the centre console where it could not really be seen by the driver!

Alfetta GTs on Sale

No sooner had the Alfetta GT been announced in May 1974 than deliveries began in earnest, first for the home and left-hand-drive European markets, then for the commercially important USA market (where Alfa's own SPICA fuel-injection system was needed for the engine to meet North America's ever-tightening exhaust emission targets, and larger energy-absorbing bumpers had to be fitted), and only then for the world's right-hand-drive territories, which of course included Great Britain.

Britain's *Autocar* magazine did not get its hands on an Alfetta GT 1.8 until October 1975. Proving right away that Alfa Romeo's original claim of a top speed of a mere 112mph (180kph) had been made to pacify the authorities in Italy (who

This was the period in motoring history when the detail of Giugiaro's styles was fascinating. The recessed filler cap and the triangular cabin air outlet vents might have been expected, but how many noticed that the profile of the hatch window was ever so slightly different from the sheet metal at the corners?

were beginning to worry about high perform-ance, accident rates, and energy consumption in general), they quoted a mean top speed of 117mph (188kph). This, at a stroke, confirmed the aerodynamic efficiency of the new style, for it bettered that of the 1750 GT Veloce, which employed precisely the same 122bhp/1,779cc engine.

One look at the right-hand-drive facia board proved that the separately positioned speedome-ter pod was not well thought through (even so, it would be several years before Alfa Romeo did anything to improve this), though it was clear that the test team liked the new car's overall package, as the initial summary confirmed: 'Exceptionally attractive coupé derivative of Alfetta saloon . . . Excellent ride, comfortable seats and very quiet when cruising. Short-legged driving position and odd instrument layout . . . Fairly expensive, but still a car to be reckoned with in this class'.

What was immediately obvious was that Alfa's decision to locate the gearbox at the rear of the car, and to link this to a technically elegant De Dion rear suspension layout, had resulted in a near-ideal weight distribution (49.1 per cent was over the driven rear wheels, close to the much-desired 50 per cent), and well-balanced road-holding:

the Alfetta GT could hardly be better balanced for two-up driving. The steering is typically Alfa in being heavier and lower-geared than one might expect. Once the weight and gearing of the steering have been accepted one can realize where it excels, which is in the way it provides exact information from the front wheels. The driver is never in any doubt what they are trying to do, and how much of a margin they have left. This excellence of feel is one of the most appealing things about the Alfetta, and goes hand in hand with roadholding of a high order. The wider tyres, compared with the saloon, give a perceptible benefit in this respect, especially in the dry when the grip can only be described as remarkable . . . The han-dling is as well-balanced as one would expect. It means that, within limits, the car handles according to the way it is driven. A late, clumsy entry to a corner

The Alfetta GT of the 1970s was a genuine, if close-coupled, four-seater car, though with only two passenger doors, access to the rear was not ideal.

In the mid-1970s, this was the original facia layout of the Alfetta GT. The theory – of separating the rev-counter from all other instruments – might have been sound (and only the single-pod instrument changed sides from left-hand to right-hand drive), but the result was visually rather awkward.

brings understeer; a slow entry and the early application of power pushes the tail wide, and a smooth, almost racing approach is rewarded with handling as near neutral as one could wish.

The downside was that the feel of the gearchange was described as 'rubbery', a trait that Alfa could never eliminate from this range of cars (the Alfetta saloon was similarly afflicted), because of the lever's remoteness from the gearbox itself, and its method of mounting. There was a basic problem here – the lever was mounted to the body shell between the seats, while the gearbox itself was supported in rubber mountings and could move slightly, both up and down on its mountings, and by several degrees of rotation about the main shaft as engine torque was randomly applied and released.

Giulietta – a Second Generation

Why is it that some car-makers stick with their most famous names, using them again and again over the years? Alfa Romeo, it seems, was so sentimental about the Giulietta, which had served it so well between 1954 and 1965, that it picked it up again in 1977.

The second-generation Giulietta was not a unique design, but was the name given to a rather sharp-edged four-door saloon, whose platform and mechanical layout were closely based on that of the Alfetta.

From 1977 to 1985, the Giulietta used the same basic floorpan, suspensions and rear-mounted transmission layout as the Alfetta saloon – both the wheelbase and track were shared between the two models – but had its own rather more sharply-defined style. It also had its own range of twin-cam engines, for the entry-level unit was a 95bhp/1,357cc version of the classic twin-cam.

Because the new Giulietta's running gear and platform was the same as that of the Alfetta, from which the Alfetta GT had already been developed, there was never any question of yet another sporting Alfa Romeo growing out of this

Even so, *Autocar* liked the car enough to summarize that:

the Alfetta sets several standards of excellence. Few would quarrel with the universal opinion of our staff that it is one of the best-looking cars one can buy for under £5,000. We can testify to the admiring looks it collects wherever it goes ... It has handling, brakes and ride to match – which is more than one can say of some more exotic machinery ...

Updates

For the first two years, of course, this model was slightly but definitely handicapped by only being available with a single – 1,779cc – engine size (except for North America, which got a detoxed 1,962cc derivative), but Alfa Romeo had always planned to flesh out the range in due course, which they did in May 1976. At the same time as the range was expanded, there were several small but timely equipment changes.

This was the point at which 1.6-litre and 2.0-litre derivatives of the same basic design – cars called Alfetta GT 1.6 and Alfetta GTV 2000 – were put on sale, but it was also the point at which the original 1.8-litre model was discontinued;

When the Alfetta GT 1.6 was added to the original 1.8-litre car in 1976, the visual differences were tiny; Alfa Romeo was not about to tell the world that this version was less powerful, after all.

The front seat/instrument panel area of the original Alfetta GT (this is a 1976-model 1.6) was not its most outstanding feature. It would be tidied up a lot in later years.

The Alfetta GTV arrived in 1976, with the well-known 2.0-litre version of the twin-cam engine. Extra brightwork in the grille was an obvious identification feature.

In the Alfetta GTV the rev-counter was red-lined at 6,000rpm, and the speedometer read up to 240kph (150mph) – stirring stuff!

21,907 had been assembled in two years, which was a very encouraging start to this car's career. It did, however, mean that the 1.8-litre Alfetta GT went down in Alfa history as having one of the shortest of all model lives, yet it had already proved to be a success.

Alfa, who were past-masters at the art of filling every possible market slot, had clearly decided that to offer three engines within 400cc of each other was sometimes counter-productive. All three engines would be offered together in saloons like the new-generation Giulietta and the Alfetta saloon, but not in the Alfetta GT.

Except for the difference in engine sizes (and power), the 1.6- and 2.0-litre cars looked, felt and sounded very similar to the original. Here is how the three cars stacked up:

Model	Engine Size	Peak Power Output
Alfetta GT 1.6	1,570cc	109bhp @ 5,600rpm
Alfetta GT 1.8	1,779cc	122bhp @ 5,500rpm
Alfetta GTV 2000	1,962cc	121bhp @ 5,300rpm

The GTV 2000's engine was actually no more powerful than the 1.8-litre had been and, accord-ing to Alfa Romeo's official figures, was *less* powerful than the engine fitted to the Giulia-based 2000 GT Veloce.

Alfa-watchers, in fact, could pick out several visual clues to the identity of the new cars:

1.6: Except for its slightly reprofiled matt-black grille, the Alfetta GT 1.6 had the same front-end as the original 1.8-litre car, along with restyled steel wheels. Inside the car, the centre console on the transmission tunnel was rearranged to pro-vide more space in the rear seats, and the hand-brake was now more neatly located. The five-speed all-indirect gearbox was as before, and was shared with the GTV 2000, but the final drive ratio had been changed to 4.3:1, which in order to compensate for a loss in engine power made the car slightly lower geared.

GTV 2000: To identify this top-of-the-range car, the grille was given a transverse pair of brightwork stripes at headlamp height, along with substantial black rubber bumper over-rid-ers, and on the rear quarters the triangular cabin air outlets had been abandoned in favour of a stylized 'GTV' logo (which still allowed air to exit, but made its own model statement at the

The Alfetta GTV 2000 had a more powerful engine than its siblings, but the styling was unchanged, except for details such as the different grille and the 'GTV' logo on the rear quarters.

From 1980 the GTV's style was retouched, to incorporate larger-section bumpers and a front spoiler, with a simpler front grille.

At the same time, the GTV's rear bumpers were made more substantial, the badge itself was changed, and a new type of cabin air extractor vent was fitted to the rear quarter.

same time). Light-alloy wheels like those of the original 1.8-litre type continued to be available (but not standard equipment); they were not even offered on the 1.6.

When *Autocar* came to test a GTV 2000 in October 1976, its earlier opinions about the 1.8-litre car were re-emphasized. In particular:

> We were disappointed by the instrument layout, which is reminiscent of some of the poorer pre-war designs ... Whatever opinion one may hold of the the square-styled faces for round dials, putting the rev-counter in the middle of the dash away from the other instruments is puzzling, and using flat glasses which reflect anything light one's companion may be wearing is simply retrograde.

A performance comparison with the early 1.8-litre car was interesting, especially as the GTV 2000's peak output was no higher than before,

and the unladen weight had only crept up by 30lb (13.6kg). The top speed of the new car was effectively the same as before (118mph vs 117mph is a trivial difference), and the 2000 accelerated only slightly faster than the 1.8-litre type: 0.5 seconds faster from rest to 60mph (96kph); 2.9 seconds to 100mph (160kph). Fuel consumption figures, too, were very similar: 23.3mpg for the GTV 2000; 23.7mpg for the 1.8-litre car.

There was no getting away from the impression, however, that the latest GTV 2000's oddities – peculiar driving position (best for the short-legged, not easy for the tall), strange instrument layout, old-fashioned heater/ventilation system, and awkward lift-up parcel shelf arrangement – could be very irritating, and Alfa seemed reluctant to take notice, or to agree to make changes. Which was a pity because, as *Autocar* concluded:

> The Alfetta GTV may sound like a not very likeable car – which couldn't be further from the truth. There

are a lot of details to criticize. But detail criticisms take more words to describe than great merits, which the Alfetta GTV has most truly, and for which it is a car to value . . . Several of its competitors are as quick in a straight line, and therefore almost as satisfying to drive, but few have such delightful steering and handling combined with such a satisfactory ride compromise . . . Another very likeable Alfa Romeo . . .

Turbodelta – an Indulgence

The Alfetta Turbodelta GTV 2.0 – launched at the Frankfurt Motor Show in September 1979, made in very small numbers, and retired early in the 1980s – was a car which many Alfa enthusiasts thought they would like to own. Yet very few took the opportunity to test drive this machine,

The GTV 2.0 Turbodelta was little more than an 'homologation special', produced with motorsport in mind. Listed only briefly in 1979 and 1980, in road-car form its 2-litre engine produced 150bhp – but more like 300bhp in motorsport trim. Very few were produced.

and even fewer seem to have ordered one. Now it is almost forgotten.

The Turbodelta, in fact, was an indulgence granted to the company's official motorsporting arm, Autodelta, so that they (not the factory at Arese) could assembly the bare minimum needed for sporting homologation, and then put the new model (which, because of the FIA's 'factor of comparison' which was applied to tur-bocharged cars, was rated at 2,747cc) into saloon car racing or into rallying. The conversion was simple enough, for unlike the other cars with which Autodelta had been connected (notably the Giulia GTA and its derivatives) there was no attempt to lighten the car by fitting light–alloy body panels. Most of the work centred around the engine, where the 1,962cc power unit of the GTV 2000 was treated to a KKK turbocharger,

The Alfetta Turbodelta engine of 1979 featured this exhaust-driven turbocharger installation on the left side of the famous twin-cam engine. In fully tuned form, underbonnet heat was tremendous.

Below: The fully prepared Turbodelta rally car looked fearsome, complete with its flared wheelarches and extra fresh-air scoops in the bonnet. With 300bhp available, it needed ultra-wide tyres to keep everything in check.

The Alfetta Turbodelta rally car looked more like an advertising man's dream than a showroom car. It looked more purposeful than it actually was. As with many other such rear-drive cars, its principal problem was a lack of traction – and competition from the four-wheel-drive Audi Quattros.

This was a one-off Alfetta Group 5 prototype, equipped with a slightly detuned V8 engine of the type first raced in 33/2 sports cars, and then used in productionized form in the Montreal.

and there were louvres in the bonnet to help release the extra underbonnet heat, along with a special paint job.

The turbocharger itself was on the left side of the engine bay, where it met the hot gases coming out of the exhaust manifold; there was an intercooler up front, close to the cooling radiator; while carburation was by a conventional pair of twin-choke Dellorto DHLA 40 types.

In 'standard' form (but how many of Autodelta's cars left the special workshops in 'standard' condition?) the engine was rated at only 150bhp, for low-compression pistons had reduced the nominal compression ratio to a mere 7.0:1, and peak boost was only 0.5bar. This, however, was not considered important by Autodelta.

For a short time Autodelta mounted a serious European Championship rally programme with Alfetta GTs, these being Jean-Claude Andruet's and Amilcare Ballestrieri's cars on their way to the Rally Costa Brava.

Hard-driven Alfetta GTs were stirring sights in European rallies, this being Leo Pittoni's car in Elba, 1975.

What mattered to them was that in fully tuned guise the engine could be boosted to no less than 300bhp at 6,000rpm, a figure which might have delivered fearsome amounts of underbonnet heat from the hard-worked turbocharger (the dispersal of which was always an enormous problem), but which made the car competitive in motorsport.

In the mid-1970s the Alfetta GT 1.8 and GTV 2000 types had built a good, if not sensational, reputation in international rallying, where drivers such as Amilcare Ballestrieri of Italy and Jean-Claude Andruet of France had been competitive at European level, if not dominant (this was the period, let us not forget, during which the mid-engined Lancia Stratos put so many other cars in the shade). Even so, Jean-Claude Andruet's 1.8-litre-engined car actually finished third in the 1975 Tour de Corse, a World Championship qualifier, behind a Lancia Stratos and a Renault-Alpine A110.

The replacement rally car, the Turbodelta, was homologated into FIA Group 4 (400 having been built, or so Autodelta claimed) in February 1980, but although this was obviously very fast, it could not compete for long in Mediterranean conditions as there often seemed to be insuperable engine overheating problems. A further sporting evolution of this car was somehow homologated in July 1980, when Autodelta convinced the authorities that it should be allowed to run its 'works' Turbodeltas with a massive fresh-air scoop in the bonnet panel, with a 221lb (100kg) lower weight limit, and with wheelarch extensions to cover extra-wide tyres. Before then, however, Turbodeltas got on to the podium of several 1980 European Championship events – including second in the Madeira, and third in the Costa Brava and Targa Florio events – but that was the height of it. The Turbodelta could not keep up with specially conceived cars like the mid-engined Renault 5 Turbos and the four-wheel-drive Audi Quattros. It was a one-season wonder.

According to Alfa Romeo and Autodelta, at least 800 were built (to meet the terms of the two sporting homologations), but these are murky waters. Alfa Romeo has never issued any separate figures, and I suspect that the true total is very much smaller. After all, when did you ever see one on the road?

This derivative, however, was always a sideshow as far as the factory was concerned, for by 1980 the Giugiaro-styled GT range of mainstream cars had become very important to Alfa Romeo. Although USA-market sales of the 2-litre cars were always somewhat disappointing – only 9,041 would be shipped across the Atlantic from 1975 to 1980 – and even though Alfa Romeo could still not shake off its rather unfair 'rust-prone' reputation, the rest of the world was obviously very happy with the larger-engined product. In 1976, the year in which the GTV 2000 was announced, 22,319 of all GT types

were built (11,210 of them being non-USA GTV 2000s), this total then edging up to 22,736 in 1977. Unhappily, this represented the peak for the Alfetta GT family, for by 1980 only 5,856 would be built in a year, that figure then only recovering once – to 8,260 – in 1980. But there was worse: although demand for the GTV 2000 had fallen away, at the same time orders for the entry-level 1.6-litre-engined car had almost evaporated.

As a 'more-show-than-go' type of car, and with a price not hugely below that of the GTV 2000, the 1.6-litre Alfetta GT had never really got established, as these year-on-year figures prove:

Alfetta GT (1.6-litre)

Year	Annual Production
1976	4,262
1977	7,935
1978	3,321
1979	787
1980	618
Total:	16,923

What was truly puzzling was that although the second energy crisis, and leap in fuel prices, hit the world in 1979 and 1980, there was no upturn in demand for a smaller-engined (and, presumably, more economical) Alfetta GT. It was no surprise, therefore, to see that when the Alfetta GT range was reshuffled yet again in 1980, the 1.6-litre type was dropped altogether.

GTV6 – the Big One

The major change to the GT range took place at the very end of 1980, when the majestic new GTV6 appeared, this being powered by Alfa's extraordinary new V6 engine. Launched only in 1979, clearly this power unit had a long career ahead of it.

Looking back, a V6 engine layout was perhaps the only one that this enterprising Italian company had not previously used. Straight engines,

The Alfetta GTV6 was still an extremely well-balanced car, the torque and flexibility of the new V6 engine turning this into quite a different sort of coupé.

When Alfa Romeo launched the Alfetta GTV6 in 1980, installing the big V6 engine meant that a new bonnet, complete with 'power bulge' was needed. Otherwise, Giugiaro's peerless style was not defiled.

the Alfasud's flat-four, flat-12s, V8s, V12s and V16s were all listed, either as road-car or as race-car types, but no V6s. As with many other of the world's major car-making companies, there had somehow never been the need, or the opportunity, to investigate V6s.

In Europe it took ages for designers and product planners to embrace such a compact layout. Lancia was a pioneer, with its Aurelia unit of 1950, and Fiat launched the Dino 206 in 1966, but these were specialized power units, and it was

Ford (Germany in 1964, UK in 1966) that finally laid down plant for long-run, mass-production V6s. By the mid-1970s the PRV (Peugeot-Renault-Volvo) 'co-operative' had also launched its own Douvrin-built V6, and the floodgates then opened.

In the 1970s Alfa knew that it needed to develop a new large engine. The famous Giulietta/Giulia/Alfetta straight-four could not be enlarged above 2 litres, while the last of the straight-six 2.6-litre engines had disappeared in

This was the GTV6 style of facia/instrument panel, which was simultaneously adopted for other Alfetta models. This time there was an integrated array of instruments, with the speedometer and rev-counter dials adjacent to each other.

This display cabin for the Alfetta GTV6 shows that, unless the front seats were pushed all the way back, there was room for four adults.

The new V6 engine was a compact 60-degree power unit, introduced in 1979, which would be used in many different Alfa Romeos in the next two decades. This was the fuel-injected version used in the GTV6.

A head-on view of the new 2.5-litre V6 engine, showing that it was compact, and almost the same size, side-by-side, as it was in length. Fuel-injection, at least, minimized the height of the fuel supply trunking.

1968. The existing Montreal V8 was really a detuned racing engine, and was not at all suitable for mass-manufacture.

On the basis that a new engine would come to have several different applications and (hopefully) would be used as a 'building block' for the next twenty years, truckloads of investment capital could finally be allocated to a new line.

Several different layouts – including straight-six types, and compact V8s – were all investigated, but in the end a series of practical imperatives led to a 60-degree V6 layout being chosen. Critically, in packaging and dimensional terms, a V6 was as broad as it was long, so if Alfa Romeo ever decided to produce a mid-engined car, or a front-wheel-drive car with a transversely-located engine, such a V6 could be realigned without upsetting the overall layout.

Various types, including different V-angles, were also analysed until, like Alfa's major rivals, a 60-degree angle was chosen as the best compromise – one that gave acceptable dynamic balance, and one that took up the least space.

Originally unveiled in April 1979, the V6 found its first home in the otherwise stodgy new

This semi-overhead study shows how neatly packaged the new V6 2.5-litre engine actually was. The unique single-overhead camshaft valve gear operating layout is concealed by the cast cylinder-head covers. In standard GTV6 form the engine produced 160bhp (DIN) at 5,600rpm.

Even though the V6 engine of the GTV6 was new, and worth boasting about, Alfa's only reaction was to insert a '2.5' badge on the tail and to fit yet another slightly different type of cast alloy road wheel.

What might have been . . . In 1974, purely as a private venture, Pininfarina styled this 'Spider' version of the Alfetta GT, with a roof panel that could be removed and stowed. There was much enthusiasm for it, but Alfa's management never allowed it to go into production.

Alfa 6 saloon, a car with totally undistinguished styling, character and road behaviour – but an excellent engine! Initially sized at 2,492cc (88mm bore × 68.3mm stroke), here was another wet-liner Alfa engine with an aluminium cylinder block, and aluminium cylinder heads with lines of opposed valves (two per cylinder) and part-spherical combustion chambers. Amazingly, though, the V6 did not have twin-cam cylinder heads. An Alfa Romeo tradition since the 1930s had had to be cast away on the grounds of cost, so as a best-alternative compromise Alfa's engineers had worked out a neat single-overhead cam installation. In each head, this featured a camshaft operating directly over the line of inlet valves, while exhaust valves were operated from that camshaft by lightweight transverse pushrods and rockers. The camshafts were driven by toothed belts from the nose of the four-bearing crankshaft.

An installation that sounded cumbersome looked far less awkward when viewed in practice, and even at this stage there was no doubt that the new power unit was free-revving, powerful, torquey, and could be persuaded to make the most spine-tingling howling noises in full-throttle use.

Here, in fact, was the beginning of a magnificent V6 dynasty of Alfa engines, for in the next two decades the capacity would be pushed out to the full 3 litres, four-valve twin-cam cylinder heads would finally be developed, and the engine would find itself positioned longitudinally and transversely in a variety of applications. Even as the twenty-first century opened, the final versions of this V6 continued to reap rave reviews from pressmen who tried them in modern Alfas. It was only the onset of Fiat-Alfa (and, soon, General Motors) rationalization that threatened its future.

In the Alfa 6 installation, this V6 actually used six downdraught single-choke Solex or Dellorto carburettors, which meant that a complex throttle linkage had to be set up very accurately for maximum performance and fuel efficiency to be assured. A fuel-injection installation would have been preferable, but cost and development time considerations ruled it out at first. This was the background to the birth of the definitive Alfetta GT, the GTV6, which made its first appearance in November 1980, a car that was centred around the new corporate V6 engine. Not that this was a straight transplant, for to complete a rejuvenation package there were other mechanical upgrades, and a much-revised facia/interior.

The engine itself was treated to Bosch L-Jetronic fuel-injection, which was not only a more elegant technical solution than a forest of carburettors, but was also likely to make for easier compliance with USA-market exhaust emission regulations. Still rated at 160bhp, the new

This is the 1980s definitive facia style used in the Alfetta GTs.

2.5-litre V6 also boasted 157lb ft of peak torque at 4,000rpm, and in this installation was a great improvement on the 2-litre 'four'. As already noted, this was a relatively wide but square and squat engine, so it fitted relatively comfortably into the existing Alfetta GTV's engine bay, except that there was now a bonnet bulge to provide sufficient clearance over the top of the V6 engine's air inlet passages. Unhappily, this new bonnet pressing included a completely useless rectangular piece of black plastic above the engine position, intended (the artists told us) to signify the presence of the V6 underneath.

To cope with the extra torque, major modifications to the transmission had been made. Working back from the engine, there were larger and more robust couplings for the two-piece propeller shaft, a twin-plate (instead of single-plate) clutch, larger bearings in the main gearbox itself, and revised internal ratios with stronger gear wheels themselves.

The chassis, similarly, had received attention, for there were larger diameter ventilated front disc brakes, firmer suspension settings and stiffer anti-roll bars, 15in (instead of 14in) road wheels, with Campagnolo alloys as standard, and 195/60-section tyres.

This was also the time at which the basic Giugiaro style was retouched, both internally and externally. On the outside of the car, most of the earlier brightwork had been eliminated in favour of black plastic, and there was a new deep and rather angular under-front-bumper spoiler, which integrated neatly with the black bumpers and the slightly flared wheelarches. Although one might have expected to see 'GTV6' logos on the rear quarters, there were none; merely a stylized outlet for cabin air.

Inside the cabin, Alfa had finally listened to the persistent storm of criticism of the original facia/instrument layout, and had made it much more conventional but, amazingly, only on left-hand-drive cars at first.

From the start on left-hand-drive cars, but only from 1982 on right-hand-drive cars, here was a layout with which any sporting driver could identify, for this time the most important

dials – the speedometer and the rev-counter – were placed together, side-by-side, ahead of the driver's eyes, the auxiliary instruments and warning lights continuing to live in the centre of the facia, above the transmission tunnel.

Except for the unique bonnet panel, the GTV 2000 also picked up the same package of exterior and interior style and equipment improvements. Some observers were irritated to see that Alfa Romeo had done nothing to improve the rear hatchback/parcel shelf/non-folding rear seat arrangements. Ford, after all, had done much better than this on the Capri since 1974, and that was a much cheaper car.

Alfetta GT Coupé Family – Production Figures

1,570cc	
GT 1.6	16,923
1,779cc	
GT 1.8	21,907
1,962cc	
GTV 2000	55,630
GTV 2000 (USA-spec)	9,041
2,492cc V6	
GTV6	17,707
GTV6 (USA-spec)	4,674
2,935cc V6	
GTV6 3.0 (South Africa only)	200
Total	126,082

Continuity in the 1980s

The GTV6 was undoubtedly a much faster and more capable coupé than its four-cylinder stablemates, which may be one reason why testers decided to carp ever more noisily over the persistent detail defects that had not been tackled. Britain's *Autocar* magazine tested a GTV6 in mid-1981, noting straight away that it still had the old-fashioned and much-derided facia layout, that the driving position was still designed for what they called the ISA (Italian Standard Ape) to enjoy, and that the gearchange quality was as rubbery as ever.

That said, here was a car that would now reach 130mph (209kph) in smooth V6-engined serenity, with 107mph (172kph) available at 6,400rpm in fourth gear; 0–60mph took only 8.8 seconds, while overall fuel consumption was a very creditable 23.2mpg.

In summary, something in the recipe of this Alfa Romeo coupé, as with so many of its predecessors, made up for everything: 'Above all, the Alfa is a car of character. On long journeys we found its faults paling into insignificance compared with the good points, one tester summing the car up as being "a marvellous companion".'

Although Alfa Romeo did not admit this until years after the range had been discontinued, the 2-litre/four-cylinder Alfetta GT model virtually died out in the early 1980s, and then only sold relatively strongly in 1983 and 1984. Three such cars were built in 1981, 174 in 1982, and a much more respectable 4,142 in 1983.

It was the GTV6, in fact, that got most of Alfa's marketing effort in that decade. With a flying start, pre-announcement, 1,179 were assembled in 1980 and a further 5,805 followed in 1981, though this was the peak of demand, which fell away gradually in the following years. Only 2,403 such cars were produced in 1985, and a mere 686 in 1986, after which it was nearly all over.

USA-market sales were respectable, although, to Alfa's accountants, no doubt disappointingly restricted. In spite of all the effort that had been put in to making the engines 'clean' and the body shells strong, a total of 9,041 four-cylinder cars and 4,674 GTV6s was the sum total of deliveries. Four-cylinder cars, in fact, were not sent to the USA after 1980, nor GTV6s after 1985.

Right at the end of the car's life, Alfa Romeo produced one oddity – a 2,935cc-engined GTV6 right-hand-drive sold exclusively in South Africa. This, please note, was a period when no mainstream enlargement of the popular V6 engine had taken place, which explains why the chosen capacity was not later replicated (all other '3-litre' types measured 2,959cc). In the case of the 'South African special', the bore was pushed

out to 93mm, the stroke to 72mm.

Such a model was produced to make the GTV6 eligible for 'showroom category' touring car racing in South African motorsport in the late 1980s, and apart from the 190bhp engine it was otherwise little different from the mainstream GTV6 models. The engine itself featured Dellorto carburettors (of original Alfa 6 type), larger valves and tubular exhaust manifolds, and special styling touches included an extra bonnet air inlet and a 3.0-litre badge on the tail.

Motorsport

In a short early/mid-1980s period in which much European touring car racing was promoted for the newly formulated Group A category (the late 1980s age of fierce Group A homologation specials such as the Ford Sierra RS500 Cosworth and the BMW M3 was still in the future), the Alfetta GTV6 proved to be surprisingly competitive. Considering that little overt effort was made by Autodelta to make this so, it was a tribute to the high-tech engineering standards and the excellent roadholding of the standard road car.

1983 was not only the first season, but an amazingly successful first season for the GTV6. In the European Touring Car Championship, not only did the GTV6s completely dominate the 2.5-litre category (by taking first to sixth places, inclusive), but this was enough to give Alfa Romeo the much-coveted Manufacturers' Championship in that year. In a Championship of twelve events, three different Alfa-mounted teams scored points, but at the end of the season it was Ronaldo Drovandi's Autodelta-prepared cars that were the most successful of all, though the Belgian 'Luigi' team's cars ran him close.

It was the same story again in 1984. Alfa Romeo GTV6s won their 2.5-litre category in every one of the twelve races, Ronaldo Drovandi's Autodelta 'works' car taking six of those successes. GTV6s took the first places in their class, which meant that Alfa Romeo once again won the Manufacturers' title. And again in 1985, making it three successful seasons. Once again it was

Drovandi's car that won the 2.5-litre category (this time with seven victories during the season), once again the GTV6s took the first five places in that category, and once again Alfa Romeo won the Manufacturers' title.

Progress, though, was so rapid that Alfa Romeo was faced with competition from more specialized new models in 1986. By this time, in any case, the company was beginning to prepare a new model (the 75) for motorsport, so there was no support for the GTV6 to go racing in future years. In the hurly-burly of European competition, though, three out of three was still a remarkable achievement.

In Britain, for the Trimoco British Saloon Car Championship, Andy Rouse (who would later become legendary for his Ford exploits) prepared Pete Hall's GTV6 so well that he won the 2.5-litre class five times, won that division convinc-

ingly, and was eventually crowned overall champion, too. Jon Dooley's car took third place in the category, and would also show well the following year when he was second in that class, with three other GTV6s close behind him.

While Rob Kirby's GTV6 won its class in the British series in 1985, and there were five other GTV6s in the top eight, the turbocharged opposition (from Ford and Nissan) was now overwhelmingly fast, and the GTV6 had come to look breathless. There would be no more British success in future years.

All this, however, was merely a creditable swansong to the career of a model which eventually died away in 1987 after more than 126,000 cars had been made. In the next few years, Alfa Romeo would only build a single type of coupé model – the Alfasud Sprint – a car that had an equally long and illustrious career.

Alfa Romeo Alfetta GT Performance

This is a summary of the figures achieved by Britain's most authoritative magazine, *Autocar*, of cars supplied for test over the years:

Model	Alfetta GT 1.8-litre	Alfetta GTV 2.0-litre	Alfetta GTV 6
	1,779cc 122bhp	1,962cc 132bhp	2,492cc 160bhp
Max speed (mph)	117	118	130
Acceleration (sec): 0–60mph	9.4	8.9	8.8
0–80mph	17.3	16.1	14.7
0–100mph	32.2	29.3	24.3
Standing G-mile (sec)	17.0	16.9	16.7
Consumption (mpg) Overall	23.7	23.3	23.2
Typical	26	26	26
Kerb weight (lb (kg))	2,393 (1,086)	2,423	2,702
Year tested	1975	1976	1981
Tested by	*Autocar*	*Autocar*	*Autocar*

7 Alfasud Sprint – Front-Wheel-Drive Flair

Only three years separated the arrival of the next generation of Alfa Romeo coupé – the Alfasud Sprint – from the Alfetta GT, but although the shape of the two cars had been influenced by Giugiaro's sure hand, technically they could not have been more different. The Alfetta GT had a classic twin-cam engine mounted up front, with a rear-mounted gearbox driving the rear wheels, whereas the Alfasud Sprint used a flat-four engine with single-cam heads, a gearbox mounted in unit with it, in an assembly that drove the front wheels.

So why and how could Alfa Romeo of Milan, a company whose entire history had been dedicated to making high-performance cars with twin-cam engines, turn to making small family cars at a factory in the south of Italy?

The answer, in a word, was 'politics'. Because Alfa Romeo had been government controlled (by the IRI) since the 1930s, and because its expansion since the 1950s had been continuous and successful, the impetus to grow further was already there. Since 1945, after all, Alfa Romeo's car-making business had been transformed from that of a company which produced only hundreds of high-priced, exclusive machines like the 6C 2500 in a year, to one which was set to produce over 100,000 Giulia-based machines every year at the end of the 1960s. Every time that price levels had come down, sales had soared.

Was further expansion possible? Was it even desirable? By the late 1960s, Alfa Romeo (and especially the IRI, who had their eye not only on profit but on employment opportunities) thought it was. The company, after all, was the second largest car-maker in Italy (although dwarfed by Fiat, Alfa was well ahead of Lancia, a

Turin-based company which was in deep financial trouble), with a huge reputation. If only, some pundits suggested, Alfa could lower their prices, they might sell more cars.

Price reductions on existing products were not feasible (this would have destroyed the meagre level of profits that were being made), but a further move towards making newly designed small-engined cars might do the trick instead. Trends in their sales of current cars already made a very telling point. Although it was exciting cars like the Giulia Sprint GTVs (and the racing GTAs) that made the headlines, it was the smaller-engined machines that sold fastest.

When this new project got underway in 1967, the following list of Alfa Romeo's current private-car production makes a telling point:

Model	Production in 1967
Giulia (1,290cc)	
– saloon	29,220
– coupé/Spider	13,020
Giulia (1,570cc)	
– saloon	20,933
– coupé/Spider	9,528
Giulia GTA	61
2600 (all types)	56
Giulia TZ	1
Total:	72,827

There is nothing obscure or misleading about these figures – more saloons were being sold than their sporty equivalents, and many more 1.3-litre types than 1.6-litre-engined types: 58 per cent instead of 42 per cent.

New Factory

This was the point when Alfa Romeo's interests and those of the Italian state came to coincide. Alfa's management dearly wanted to develop a new model – a smaller model, a cheaper model – while the IRI wanted them to do the same. But there was a snag. Alfa Romeo wanted to expand, felt they had space around the Arese plant to do so, but found this blocked by their backers. The IRI, on the other hand, was happy to see Alfa Romeo expand, but wanted to see this done in a region of high unemployment. Although there was plenty of work available in the north of Italy, which was booming, it was in the south that jobs were hard to find. The solution – easy for politicians to make, but difficult for hard-headed businessmen like Alfa Romeo to accept – was that Alfa Romeo was directed to build its new model in a new factory in the south. (The same type of coercion was applied to British car-makers in the 1950s, resulting in new factories in Scotland and on Merseyside, of which only two have survived to this day.)

Alfa dug in its heels, complained, begged and pleaded, but in the end was forced to concede. In the end, they agreed to develop a brand new industrial complex at Pomigliano d'Arco, close to Naples, where everything connected with the new car – pressings, body assembly, engine and transmission assembly – would be concentrated. Thus the Alfasud (Alfa Romeo South) project was born.

There was one consolation, though. As far as Alfa Romeo was concerned, at least this project would not have to be carried out on virgin territory, for they had a good deal of previous experience of this site. Pomigliano d'Arco was already the site of a smaller element of the company's business, one which had made aircraft engines during the Second World War (until September 1943, when it was over-run by Allied forces), and one which had an airfield attached.

Finance, at least, was not going to be a problem, for in 1967, when the project took off, it was decided to spend £200 million on the new complex (6 per cent came as a government grant, 44 per cent was a long-term loan from the government, the rest coming from Alfa's own resources). Physical space was not a limiting factor either. Even in Phase 1 of its evolution, the Alfasud complex was theoretically able to produce 300,000 cars a year, though the company cautiously only hoped to build 175,000 of the first new models.

Steel sheet (for body panels), major engine and transmission castings and forgings would all be supplied from the north, but the majority of the new complex would be virtually self-contained. A test track (utilizing some of the redundant airfield facilities) would be developed alongside the factory buildings.

With construction work starting in April 1968, for completion in 1970–71, and with a huge untapped source of (admittedly, unskilled) labour close by, this factory was scheduled to

---

Alfasud – the Pomigliano d'Arco Project

According to all industrial logic, Alfa Romeo should have kept the new-technology Sud project close to its traditional HQ in the Milan area. Unfortunately, Alfa was still controlled by the Istituto Ricostruzione Industriale – effectively, they operated as a nationalized concern – and lacked their own free will. They could not even consider tackling this project without taking on state-provided finance, and the political pressures that went with it.

In the late 1960s, Italy's politicians had to face up to the fact that in the south of the country – effectively, anywhere south of Rome – there was a desperate shortage of jobs. As a result, the IRI directed Alfa Romeo to develop its new factory in that part of the world.

Since Alfa Romeo's aircraft engine division, and an adjacent airfield for flight test operations, had been set up at Pomigliano d'Arco, just north-east of Naples, in the 1930s (after the Second World War the buildings had been redeveloped for the local assembly of Renault Dauphine cars), this site was considered satisfactory for the development of a new factory. Yet this spacious area, which was almost under the shadow of Vesuvius, was a considerable distance – about 850km (530 miles) – from Milan.

build 500 new cars every day in 1972, and up to 1,000 a day was thought to be possible.

New Thinking

Design work on the new car, the Series 901A, which to emphasize its novelty adopted an entirely new type of Alfa Romeo chassis numbering prefixed by AS (for Alfasud), began in 1967 under the direction of Rodolfo Hruska, the Austrian-born engineer who already had a long record of success at Alfa Romeo, dating back to 1951.

For the first time since the design of the Giulietta in the mid-1950s, Alfa Romeo could once again start with the proverbial 'clean slate'. Because this project was meant to offer smaller and more affordable Alfa Romeos than ever before, there were no forced (or even voluntary) carry-over parts from the larger Giulia range.

Within an estimated overall length of 157in (4,000mm), and with a 96.6in (2,455mm) wheelbase, on a commonized but very versatile new chassis platform, the team set out to develop the two-door and four-door saloons which would appear first (and which would always make up the majority of Alfasud sales), estate car derivatives, and the sporty coupés. An open-top Spider was postulated, but nothing ever came of that.

In terms of its timing, the project kept to schedule, for the first prototype saloons ran in 1968, development proceeded smoothly, and the company was ready to unveil the first cars at the Turin Motor Show in November 1971. Even so, deliveries in series would not begin until mid-1972, and the sporty Sprint would not actually be announced until 1976.

With no restrictions as to 'custom and practice' from the older models, Hruska and his team soon concluded that they wanted to develop a front-engined, front-wheel-drive platform, and in certain respects it was similar to that which Citroën also put on sale as the GS model. Not only did this layout make the best economic and dynamic sense, but the packaging possibilities were favourable, and as all the major running gear was concentrated ahead of the toeboard, it made it even easier for a whole range of different body styles to be developed.

They briefly resurrected the single Tipo 103 prototype of 1960 (*see* Chapter 4), studied it once again, but soon discarded it as obsolete, too large, too heavy and – certainly – too ugly. The stage was then set for a new approach.

Right from the start (there is little evidence that any other layout was ever seriously considered), the Alfasud took shape around a flat-four

Rodolfo Hruska – Sud Pioneer

Although he will always be known as the 'father of the Alfa Sud', Rodolfo Hruska had a long and distinguished career in the motor industry, much of it with Alfa Romeo.

Born in Vienna, Austria, in 1915, he graduated as an engineer in 1935. Then, in 1938, he joined the Porsche Bureau in Stuttgart, where he worked on vehicles as diverse as the original VW Beetle and the Tiger tank.

From 1946 he became involved in the Porsche-designed Cisitalia Grand Prix project, moving to Turin in 1947 to oversee the construction of that advanced single-seater. When the project closed down he was soon invited to become a consultant to Alfa Romeo, on productionizing the 1900 family car project. After becoming Technical Manager in 1954, he moved up to General Assistant Director in 1956.

Then came a sojourn away from Milan – from 1959 to 1967 he held high office at Simca in France, while liaising with Fiat in Turin. Returning to Alfa Romeo in 1967, he became Managing Director/General Manager of the SICA project, which embraced all technical aspects of the new Alfa Sud, and only a year later he took control of the entire Alfa Sud project, which included the building of the new factory at Pomigliano d'Arco.

Further promotion then followed, for in 1974 Hruska took over responsibility for the design and development of the entire Alfa Romeo range, a task which, until his retirement, embraced the Sud, the Alfetta, and the 33, 75 and 90 models which gradually evolved from them.

The first of the Alfasuds to be announced, in November 1971, was this very conventional-looking front-wheel-drive saloon car with a choice of two-door or four-door accommodation.

The first high-performance Alfasud was the TI saloon, which appeared in 1974. It was the first in the range to use the five-speed gearbox, which would be standard in all Sprints.

The Alfasud chassis layout, seen here in a 'ghosted' saloon, would be used in its entirety under the Sprint's shell. Features included a flat-four engine and front-wheel drive.

engine mounted ahead of the line of the front wheels, which was in unit with the final drive, this having a four-speed gearbox positioned behind it. Even at the 'paper-project' stage, the team allowed for a 1.5-litre engine and a five-speed gearbox, even though the first production cars had only 1,186cc and four forward speeds!

Compared with 'traditional' Alfa engines, it was not only the flat-four layout that was novel (the only previous 'flat' Alfa engines had been prototype Grand Prix engines in the 1940s and 1950s), but the fact that it had a cast-iron cylinder block and single-overhead-camshaft valve gear, the cams being driven by internally cogged belt from the crankshaft itself. In its original 63bhp/1,186cc form, it was also considerably oversquare (80mm bore × 59mm stroke), and was the very first Alfa power unit ever to be configured like that.

Suspension installations, too, were novel – to

Flat-Four Engines

Although Alfa's flat-four Sud engine was new to them in 1971, it was already a well-established layout in the motor industry. Flat-fours – those with cylinders opposed to each other at either side of a common crankshaft – had been around for decades, especially as they could be made low, unobtrusive and compact.

In the 1930s, Steyr, Tatra, Jowett and – most notably – VW all built cars with flat-four layouts. After the war it was VW (and, closely related, Porsche) who made the layout so famous.

It is, I am sure, significant that the 'father' of the Alfa Sud, Rudolfo Hruska, worked for the Stuttgart-based Porsche Bureau in the late 1930s, when that company was heavily involved in the original VW project.

Although millions of Alfa Romeo flat-four engines would be built (the last of this type were fitted to Alfa Romeo 145s and 146s in the mid-1990s), it was abandoned when the effects of post-Fiat takeover rationalization began to be felt.

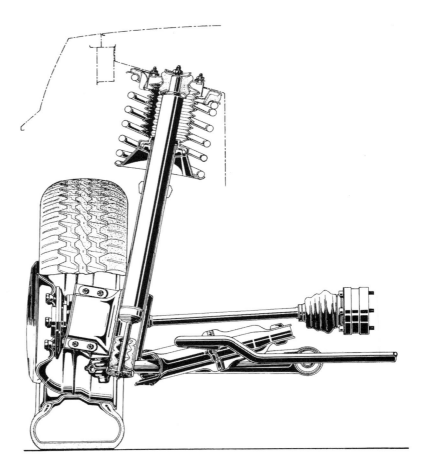

The Alfasud Sprint used simple, effective, MacPherson strut front suspension. The brakes are not visible because on this model they were mounted inboard, between the drive shafts and the transaxle casing.

Alfa Romeo at least, though each and every feature had previously been seen on other makes and models of car. At the front there was a conventional coil spring/MacPherson strut layout, with a wide-based lower wishbone, and the front disc brakes mounted inboard at each side of the transmission casing, allied to rack-and-pinion steering, which was positioned high, above the transaxle and behind the line of the flat-four engine. Tyres of 145-13in radial ply were standard.

At the rear there were other novelties – a sturdy fabricated axle beam (there was no final drive unit) to keep the wheels vertical, this being sprung on combined coil spring/damper units, and located by in-line Watts linkages and a transversely positioned Panhard rod. The beam itself acted as a huge, ultra-stiff anti-roll bar. In this case, naturally, the disc brakes were outboard at the wheel hubs. And because there was no need to make provision for a propeller shaft under the centre line of the floor, as a final layout novelty the fuel tank was mounted low, wide and ahead of the line of the rear axle beam.

For a small-engined 'family car' this was a remarkably audacious arrangement of the running gear, though, given the free hand which Hruska's team had been granted to work it up, this was no less than might have been expected from them. It wasn't long before testers, pundits and the general public realized that it was also a well-balanced chassis, with crisp steering, great front-wheel-drive handling, and the sort of balance that cried out for more horsepower and a more sporting image.

Front-Wheel-Drive Influences

Nowadays, front-wheel-drive is the norm – every early-2000s Alfa Romeo road car drives through its front wheels – but until the 1960s it was a rarity. In the 1930s it was Citroën, in the 1940s Saab, then in the 1950s there was DKW, but it was the arrival of BMC's transverse-engined Mini in 1959 which made all the difference. Renault followed up with the R4 hatchback, then came BMC's 1100, Ford-of-Germany's Taunus 12M – and the floodgates opened.

The Italian industry, where rear-engined cars like the Fiat 500 and 600 types were selling in huge numbers, took time to change direction. One influence was the fact that Innocenti began making BMC cars under licence, but from 1964 Autobianchi (a Fiat-owned company) began building front-wheel-drive Primulas. Fiat then followed up with the 128 and 127 models, after which there was no going back.

The European trend to front-wheel drive therefore became unstoppable for those makers wanting to produce new small- and medium-engined machinery. Alfa Romeo, in fact, had studied then built a 900cc transverse-engined front-wheel-drive prototype – the Tipo 103 – in 1960, but had sidelined it in favour of developing a larger new model, the Giulia.

When project work on the new Alfasud model began in 1967, the Tipo 103 was briefly studied again, then discarded. The Alfa Sud, therefore, was to be all-new, from stem to stern.

By contrast, the style of the saloon car derivative was neither advanced nor startling. Even though its shape and packaging had been developed by the Giugiaro/Ital Design office – this actually pre-dated the work Giugiaro would carry out on the Alfetta GT (*see* Chapter 6) – it was merely neat, rounded and practical. Only a four-door saloon would be offered at first, the higher-powered two-door derivative not following until late 1973, and the estate car ('Giardinetta') in 1975.

Sprint – 'Patience, Please'

The development of a more powerful, faster, and sportily-styled coupé version of the Alfasud – naturally enough it was to be titled 'Sprint' – had always been foreseen, but it was a long time before there was any sight of such a car. Although Giugiaro/Ital Design had started work on it by 1970, the Alfasud Sprint was not unveiled until September 1976.

One reason for this was that in the first few years of its existence the fact is that the Alfasud project stumbled from crisis to crisis (industrial relations problems and quality control deficiencies being foremost), and never operated profitably, primarily because the Pomigliano d'Arco factory suffered from chronic absenteeism among its workforce. Other noted Alfa-watchers have

pointed out that this was one of the reasons why Alfa Romeo had never really wanted to set up shop in southern Italy. One expert has even written that:

> Others pointed to the slow pace of life in the South, the tradition of working only sufficiently to bring in money for a comfortable but unambitious lifestyle, and then relaxing and taking a break without warning ... Certainly, industrial relations, aggravated by the local politics, proved to be highly intractable problems from the very beginning, and instead of the initial target of 'only' 175,000 cars for the first year of production, less than half of that number – 78,000 in all – actually left the factory.

It just so happened, too, that the Alfasud Sprint was not announced until the last of the Giulia-based coupés (the 1300 GT Junior/1600 GT Junior/2000 GT Veloce models described in Chapter 4) had been produced at Arese. Neat and convenient, if not commercially striking.

In the meantime, the running gear under Alfasud saloons had progressively been improved, to make it more suitable for use under the Sprint's style, for no-one, surely, would have been interested in a 63bhp/1.2-litre/four-speed car. First of all, in 1974, the 1.2-litre engine was boosted to 68bhp, then a five-speed gearbox was ready in 1976 and, best of all, the first enlargement of the

Alfasud Sprint family (1977–89, all types)

Layout

Unit-construction body-chassis structure, with steel panels. Two-door, front engine/front drive, sold as 2+2-seater coupé model.

Engine

Block material	Cast iron
Head material	Cast aluminium
Cylinders	4 in horizontally-opposed layout
Cooling	Water
Main bearings	3
Valves	2 per cylinder, operated by single-overhead camshafts and inverted bucket-type tappets, driven by internally cogged belt from crankshaft

1,286cc: bore and stroke 80 × 64mm; compression ratio 9.0:1; one downdraught twin-choke Weber DIR/6 carburettor; 75bhp (DIN) @ 6,000rpm, 76lb ft @ 3,200rpm

1,351cc: bore and stroke 80 × 67.2mm; compression ratio 9.0:1; one downdraught twin-choke Weber DIR/61 carburettor; 79bhp (DIN) @ 6,000rpm, 81lb ft @ 3,500rpm

1,351cc Sprint Veloce: bore and stroke 80 × 67.2mm; compression ratio 9.75:1; two downdraught twin-choke Weber carburettors; 86bhp (DIN) at 5,800rpm, 87.5lb ft @ 4,000rpm

1,490cc: bore and stroke 84 × 67.2mm; compression ratio 9.0:1; one downdraught twin-choke Weber DIR/61 carburettor; 85bhp (DIN) @ 6,000rpm, 98lb ft @ 3,500rpm

1,490cc Sprint Veloce: bore and stroke 84 × 67.2mm; compression ratio 9.5:1; twin downdraught twin-choke Weber carburettors; 95bhp (DIN) @ 5,800rpm, 96lb ft @ 4,000rpm

1,490cc Green Cloverleaf: bore and stroke 84 × 67.2mm; compression ratio 9.5:1; twin downdraught twin-choke Weber carburettors; 105bhp (DIN) @ 6,000rpm, 98lb ft @ 4,000rpm

1,717cc: bore and stroke 87 × 72.2mm; compression ratio 9.5:1; two downdraught twin-choke Weber carburettors; 118bhp (DIN) @ 5,800rpm, 109lb ft @ 3,500rpm

1,717cc, with catalyst (for use with unleaded fuel): bore and stroke 87 × 72.2mm; compression ratio 9.5:1; Bosch LE-Jetronic fuel-injection; 105bhp (DIN) @ 5,500rpm, 107lb ft @ 4,500rpm

Transmission

Five-speed all-synchromesh manual gearbox

Clutch	Single dry plate; hydraulically operated

Internal Gearbox Ratios

[Ratios from 1982–83 in square brackets]

Top	0.931	[0.825]
4th	1.115	[1.027]

3rd	1.434	[1.387]
2nd	2.062	[2.05]
1st	3.545	[3.75]
Reverse	3.091	[3.091]
Final drive	4.11:1 (1,286cc); 3.89:1 (1,351cc and 1,490cc); 3.7:1 (1,717cc)	

Suspension and Steering

Front	Independent, coil springs, MacPherson struts, lower wishbones, anti-roll bar, telescopic dampers incorporated in struts
Rear	'Dead' (beam) axle, by coil springs, twin Watts linkages, Panhard rod, telescopic dampers
Steering	Rack and pinion
Tyres	165/70 SR–13 radial-ply (185/60HR–14 with 1,717cc)
Wheels	Cast alloy disc, bolt-on
Rim width	5.0in (1300), 5.5in (other models)

Brakes

Type	Disc brakes at front and rear, hydraulically operated (rear drums, 1987)
Size	10.5in dia. front discs, 9.2in dia. rear discs

Dimensions

Track	
Front	54.7in (1,389mm); 55.0in (1,395mm) (1,351/1,500/1,717cc)
Rear	53.5in (1,359mm); 53.7in (1,365mm) (1,351/1,500/1,717cc)
Wheelbase	96.6in (2,455mm)
Overall length	155.0in (3,937mm)
Overall width	63.8in (1,621mm)
Overall height	51.0in (1,295mm)
Unladen weight	1,907lb (865kg) (1,286cc) to 2,150lb (975kg) (1,717cc)

The Alfasud engine was a flat-four design, with single-overhead camshaft valve gear. For the original 1.3-litre Sprint of 1976, only one carburettor was fitted, which meant that the inlet passages were long and tortuous.

engine – to 1,286cc and 75bhp – was also finalized.

The scene was set for the launch of the Alfasud Sprint, and for the delivery of the first 2,192
cars before the end of 1976. It caused a real stir,
for by comparison with any other model in the
Alfasud range, it was very beautiful, fast, and had
genuine sporty star quality.

Hruska's team, of course, took all the credit for
the chassis, but once again it was Giorgetto Giugiaro's Ital Design team that had worked a miracle with the style. Here, on the same wheel-

*The Alfasud Sprint
used the same
platform as the
saloons, but was
graced by an
extremely elegant
hatchback/coupé
style by Giorgetto
Giugiaro.*

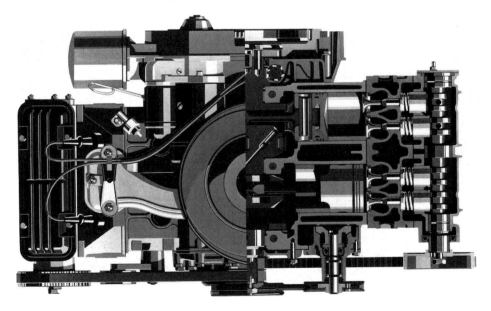

*This cross-section
view of the Sud
Sprint engine shows
that the cylinders
were widely
separated, and the
valves were vertical
and side-by-side in
the cylinder heads.*

base/platform as the other Suds (which meant that the rear wheels were set well back towards the tail panel), was a crisply styled sporty hatchback, which combined the Sud's well-liked front-drive chassis with the promise of 100mph (160kph) performance, and styling that was defi-

nitely (and intentionally) related to that of the costly and more glamorous Alfetta GT.

Above the all-important platform, every panel and body sub-assembly of the Sprint was unique. More angular in its detail than the Sud saloon, the Sprint was 2in longer, marginally wider, but had

All Alfasuds were two-door 2+2-seater types, with comfortable and well-shaped front seats, though even with fold-down backrests the access to the rear was not easy.

The three-quarter rear view of the Sud Sprint body style shows the mainly glass hatchback, and the very high rear sill, which made loading the boot rather awkward.

a roof line which was 3in lower. This body shell envelope, and the combination of a steeply sloping roof line behind the line of the front seats, made this a 2+2-seater at best.

But no-one was complaining, for that long and shapely tail included a lift-up glass hatchback (Alfetta GT-style), yet this time, unlike the Alfetta GT (*see* Chapter 6), there was neither a hatch support strut nor a lift-up parcel shelf to get in the way of its usefulness. Instead, there was a fixed position parcel shelf which could be rolled forward to reveal the boot space underneath. One snag, however, was that the hatchback only opened down to car-waist-line level (the lower line of the side windows), which meant that the rear sill was very high, and not at all convenient if heavy or awkward loads had to be stowed. But this was a sporty car, Alfa commented, so who cares?

In all other ways, too, Alfa Romeo had clearly thought about this car, and the image they wanted to present. The style, on its own, looked right, especially when one considered the four-headlamp nose, so closely and obviously similar to the Alfetta GT, and even more so when one inspect-

ed the neat facia/instrument panel layout, complete with a steering column that was adjustable for rake, which was as welcoming and logical as the Alfetta GT was an ergonomic mess.

The cabin actually carried no better than a 2+2 layout, for compared with the Alfasud saloons both the rear legroom and headroom were restricted, and since this was only a two-door machine, access to the rear compartment was limited. It was, however, fully competitive with similar coupés of the day – in Italy, notably, the Fiat 128 3P, and in Germany the VW Scirocco coupé.

It had all the hallmarks of the best sort of sporty Alfa, too – the sharply cut-off tail, the built-in chin spoiler under the front bumper, and the quadrifoglio badge on the flanks. It also had nicely styled wheels and that four-square stance which positively told the world: don't mess with me, I can handle any treatment you give to me!

The latest chassis, engine and running gear were a driver's delight, and made the Sprint immensely satisfying to drive. The newly enlarged 1,286cc engine was powerful and torquey, the five-speed gearbox's ratios were well

In the mid-1970s Alfa was proud to display a selection of its latest models on the grass outside the administrative HQ at Arese, near Milan. The Alfasud Sprint is at front left, while the Alfetta GT is centre right; the family resemblance is clear.

matched to it, and the handling (aided by new, wider-section 165/70-13in radial ply tyres) was well up to the mark.

Perhaps it was Alfa's determination to make the body shell of this hatchback as rigid as that of the saloons, and the loading up with an extra 70lb (32kg) of cabin sound-deadening material, which led to the original Sprint being about 84lb (38kg) heavier than the saloon. Yet it was still a very spritely little car. A 100mph+ (160kph+) top speed, linked to 0–60mph sprints in around thirteen seconds, meant that here was a car that could match the Giulia-based GT 1300 Junior (and so it should, as it was a more compact car) – and it enjoyed that marvellous front-wheel-drive handling, too.

A Long Career

Following the September 1976 launch, deliveries from Pomigliano d'Arco began almost at once, with 2,192 cars rolling off the assembly line before the end of that year, and a further 12,046 following in 1977.

This, though, was only the start of a long, successful and complicated career, for between 1976 and 1979, no fewer than 121,434 Sprints of all types would be built, in 1.3-, 1.5- and 1.7-litre flat-four-engined forms, with peak power ratings varying from 75bhp/1,286cc to no less than 118bhp/1,717cc. Technically, the only lasting disappointment was that the launch of the much-revised 16-valve twin-cam-headed version of the engine (in April 1988) came too late to benefit the Sprint.

All this, several trim packs, and other special editions (some only sold in one particular territory), made enough headlines to keep demand buoyant until the late 1980s – and they make the Sud Sprint as difficult to summarize as any other sporting Alfa.

Throughout that time, however, no major facelift was ever carried out (in American terms, no 'sheet metal' was ever changed), nor were engine transplants of any other type carried out. In chassis terms, the only significant change came in the mid-1980s, when moves to rationalize with the Alfa 33 (the replacement model which

took over from the Sud) resulted in rear wheel disc brakes being dropped in favour of (theoretically less effective) drums.

The best way to follow this evolution is to highlight each new derivative as it appeared.

Sprint 1350

When Alfa Romeo enlarged the Sud's base engine to 1,351cc (the stroke went up to 67.2mm, compared with 59mm in the original 1.2-litre engine), it was almost inevitable that the Sprint would follow suit. Accordingly, from August 1978, and as a direct replacement for the original Sprint 1.3, the Sprint 1350 took over. Peak power and peak torque both rose, modestly, by 4bhp and 5lb ft, respectively. There had been no style or important chassis changes.

This model, however, was short-lived, and would itself give way to the range of 1.5-litre-engined cars at the end of 1979.

Sprint 1.5

In many ways the 1.5-litre-engined car which first appeared in August 1978 was the definitive Alfasud Sprint that we had all been waiting for since the early 1970s – a time when the car itself was known to be under development, and the enlarged engines had become an open secret.

Here was the flat-four engine the engineering team had always envisaged (and for which space had always been laid out in the cylinder block), and for which the chassis had always been ready. In this case, engine enlargement had been achieved by increasing the bore to 84mm, while retaining the crankshaft of the 1,351cc derivative. Yet although the engine produced 85bhp – 57bhp/litre – it was still only in a modest state of tune, with a single downdraught Weber carburettor and long, sinuous inlet passages.

Road tests showed a top speed of 103mph (165kph), with 0–60mph acceleration now available in 11.2 seconds. They also showed that this was a more capable all-round car than the original 1.3-litre had ever been, and that Alfa's sporty character was still there in abundance.

As *Autocar* testers commented:

> The Alfasud Sprint is undeniably a sports coupé, civilized yet fun, and since like all the handsome Alfas it has not been styled by Alfa Romeo themselves, it is to most eyes very pretty and looks the part… The characteristic Alfasud exhaust sizzle is there, not quite too loud, and complementing the delightfully eager character of the engine. Response is excellent; there are no disagreeable flat spots … The extra 204cc, those 10 more bhp and perhaps most importantly for normal use, the 11 per cent increase in maximum torque together add up to a very worthwhile improvement in performance – something which the Alfasud chassis has long cried out for.

Although it would soon be overshadowed by yet more powerful versions of the model, the 'basic' 1.5-litre version of the Sprint would carry on in production, strongly until 1983, and finally until 1985.

Sprint Veloce 1.3

In 1980, starting up what Alfa Romeo's own records call the 'Series III' Alfasuds (this was not a widely advertised nomenclature), the company introduced two closely linked 'Sprint Veloce' versions – this version with the latest 1,351cc engine, and another (*see page 171*) with the larger 1,490cc engine.

The Sprint Veloce 1.3 was not made available in every market, though for fiscal (taxation) reasons it was popular in its native Italy. In fact it sold slowly – only 3,801 such types were produced between 1980 and 1982 – but as a 'tax-cheater' it presumably served its purpose.

In this case, the 1,351cc engine had been boosted, not only by having a 9.75:1 compression ratio – the highest that would figure in this engine – but with the fitment of twin downdraught dual-choke Weber carburettors and efficient manifolding (which suddenly made the power unit look more purposeful), it peaked at no less than 86bhp (DIN) at 5,800rpm, which was almost exactly the same rating as the non-Veloce 1.5-litre car.

Sprint Veloce 1.5

The 1.5-litre-engined Sprint Veloce was an altogether more serious and successful project, of

The Sprint Veloce 1.5, with 95bhp, went on sale in 1980.

By 1986 the 1.5-litre-engined Sprint Veloce had lost some of the styling purity of the original, though the near-110mph (176kph) performance was never compromised.

which no less than 13,854 were built in the first year (1980).

Visually, the engine looked the same as the smaller 1,351cc type, complete with twin dual-choke Webers, but even though the compression ratio was limited to 9.5:1, the help of the wider cylinder bore allowed 95bhp to be developed. Not only that, but peak torque of 96lb ft was no less than 26 per cent better than had been seen in the original 1.3-litre-engined Sprint of 1976.

In other words, this was fast becoming a more broad-chested, flexible and effective sports coupé, for top speed was now nudging 110mph (176kph) (this could certainly be bettered in even slightly favourable wind conditions – this was not the most aerodynamically-shaped body in the world!).

Tiny style changes, mostly decorative, such as

in the use of black-finish door pillars and the chrome name badge on the tail gate, with the use of delicately detailed alloy road wheels, made many people think that this was the final and definitive Sud Sprint coupé – but they were wrong. A further boost to the 1.5-litre engine, and the introduction of an enlarged engine (the final enlargement, as it happens), were on the way.

Sprint 1.5 Green Cloverleaf

The next significant change came in the spring of 1983, when Alfa Romeo once again juggled all its resources, and its bag of model names, badges and preferences. The result was a car called the 1.5 'Green Cloverleaf' (*Quadrifoglio Verde*), which was effectively a special-edition version of the 1.5 Sprint Veloce.

Giorgetto Giugiaro's Ital Design concern shaped both the Sud Sprint 1.5 Green Cloverleaf (left) and the Alfetta GTV6 (right) in the early 1970s, their styles being timeless, and still looking good in the early 1980s.

The original Sud Sprint was a 76bhp/1,286cc-engined car, which was made in various guises from 1976 to 1989. This was a 1985 model, with the latest protective cappings on the flanks.

The Sud Sprint Green Cloverleaf of the early 1980s (this is a 1984−85 model) had a 105bhp/1,490cc engine and these very smart alloy wheels. The general style was the same as it had always been since this model was unveiled in 1976.

Once again, this was a variation on a familiar theme, for there were no major style changes, though the shield grille and a line along the side of the car were both picked out in green. Since the bumpers and the stripe along the sides were both black, and there was almost a complete absence of brightwork, this was definitely an understated model.

Enthusiasts, however, were delighted to see that there had been yet another boost to the flat-four engine's power output. Still with its 9.5:1 compression ratio, and still with twin down-draught dual-choke Weber carburettors, helped along by a series of top-end engine and porting changes, and revised camshaft profiles, it had been further developed and now produced no less than 105bhp at 6,000rpm. Important chassis modifications included the stiffening up of the suspension, and yet another alloy wheel style, allied to wide, squat, metric-measure Michelin TRX tyres of 190/55HR-340.

Without question, this was the sportiest and most purposeful Sud Sprint so far, though the humdrum aerodynamic qualities of the body shell kept the top speed stubbornly under 110mph (176kph). Even so, the design was perhaps beginning to show its age (more recently announced rivals had set new standards), as *Autocar* testers noted in 1984: 'The Sprint Green Cloverleaf is a useful improvement upon the previous Sprint, its only real drawbacks being the awkward seating position and a fair degree of mechanical noise. On the plus side, you get a responsive little coupé which, in our opinion, is still the best-looking in the class.'

The public, need I say, loved this car, for with no fewer than 9,695 built in its first year, 1983, it was by far the best-selling Sud Sprint of this and future years. It was not dropped until the end of 1987, when it was replaced by the final, 1.7-litre car.

The Sprint 1.5 Green Cloverleaf was one of the best-specified of all Sud Sprint types. It could be identified by the green piping around the grille shield, on the ridges of the black plastic bumpers, and along the flanks.

Sprint 1.7

The ultimate Sprint was introduced in the winter of 1987–88, when the 1,717cc-engined versions – Sprint and Sprint Veloce – were put on sale. The two cars were mechanically identical, and both shared a new transverse rear spoiler at the bottom edge of the glassback tailgate, along with yet another style of alloy wheels (14in diameter, with 185/60R14 tyres), the difference between them being that the Sprint Veloce had an extra body kit which comprised side skirts and a larger front spoiler.

This was an engine that had already been blooded in the 33 saloon, and was absolutely the largest capacity that could be squeezed out of this particular flat-four layout.

To gain this final 'stretch' – from 1,490cc to 1,717cc, no less than 15 per cent (the engine's capacity now being 45 per cent larger than it had been in 1971) – the design engineers had been obliged to change the cylinder block casting, for the new engine had a wider bore and a signifi-

cantly longer stroke. For the very first time, too, this flat-four derivative had hydraulic tappets (not needed, or wanted, even, in the Sprint chassis), because this engine package had been evolved for the Sud-based 33 model, and its planned replacements.

Here, in fact, was an engine that had made great strides over the years, as its 'first and last' Sud Sprint specifications show:

Feature	Sprint 1300 (1976)	Sprint 1.7 (1988)
Capacity	1,286cc	1,717cc
Bore	80mm	87mm
Stroke	64mm	72.2mm
Peak power	75bhp (DIN)/ 6,000rpm	118bhp (DIN)/ 5,800rpm

The Alfa Romeo 33, introduced in 1983, was a bigger and altogether more civilized car than the Alfasud, but used much of the same chassis and platform details. Some thirty-three features (including the rear drum brakes, a retrograde step) were eventually added to the late-model Sprints.

The final upgrading of the Sud Sprint came in 1988, with the launch of the 118bhp/1,717cc version of the engine; the new rear spoiler was a feature. Here was a car that would approach 115mph (185kph) and had great character.

The Sprint 1.7 Veloce of 1988–89 was mechanically identical to other 1.7-litre-engined Sprints, but was distinguished by its extra body kit, which included a deeper front spoiler, side skirts, and special five-spoke road wheels.

Although this was still a car with many small but irritating faults (the driving position, the curious lack of self-centring action in the steering, the high rear loading sill, the poor aerodynamics, and the high fuel consumption which went hand-in-hand with it), the 1.7 was nevertheless the most capable Sud Sprint of them all.

Here, at last, was a Sud Sprint which went as well as its specification suggested that it should – the top speed being 114mph (183kph) (and

107mph (172kph) available at the 6,200rpm rev limit in fourth gear), with 0–60mph finally available in less than ten seconds – 9.5 seconds being a typical result.

Although 663 of these 1.7-litre-engined Sprints were produced before the end of 1987, and a very creditable 4,212 followed in 1988, by that time the Sud Sprint was beginning to look, and feel, old-fashioned.

Alfa Romeo Alfasud Sprint Performance

This is a summary of the figures achieved by Britain's most authoritative magazine, *Autocar*, over the years:

Model	Alfasud Sprint 1.5	Alfasud Sprint Green Cloverleaf	Alfasud Sprint 1.7
	1,490cc 85bhp	1,490cc 105bhp	1,717cc 118bhp
Max speed (mph)	103	107	114
Acceleration (sec)			
0–60mph	11.2	10.8	9.5
0–80mph	20.8	20.1	16.8
0–100mph	–	42.6	33.2
Standing ¼-mile (sec)	18.6	18.0	17.6
Consumption (mpg)			
Overall	25.1	23.9	25.7
Typical	28	26	28
Kerb weight (lb (kg))	2,040 (925)	2,148 (974)	2,148 (974)
Year tested	1978	1984	1988
Tested in	*Autocar*	*Autocar*	*Autocar*

Alfasud Sprint Family – Production Figures

1,286cc	
Sprint	25,330
Sprint Veloce	3,801
1,351cc	
Sprint	2,839
1,490cc	
Sprint	30,576
Sprint Veloce	31,934
Sprint Green Cloverleaf	21,783
1,717cc	
Sprint and Sprint Veloce	4,921
Total	121,184

After slumping badly after the onset of the second energy crisis in 1979–80, sales of all types surged back, to peak again (at 14,690) in 1983. The slide then began – to 5,668 in 1984, to 3,938 in 1985, then pottered on to no more than 5,023 in 1988. Only fifty-four cars were produced in the first month of 1989, after which Alfa Romeo pulled the plug, bringing this attractive little car to an end.

With the parent company now in transition – Fiat had taken control at the end of 1986 – and with the pragmatists suggesting that it was four-door saloons, not sporty coupés, which were the key to future profits, was this the last-ever Alfa Romeo coupé?

Takeover by Fiat

Although the IRI (the state-financed operation that had controlled Alfa Romeo from 1933) had always been supportive, by the 1980s its patience was wearing thin. Political pressure had obliged it to back the assembly of the Alfasud family in the Naples area, a much-hyped link-up with Nissan (the Arna project) had been a sales disaster, and the mood of the country suggested that it was time for the IRI to cut its ties and walk away.

The word went around, and one of the first giants to pick up the scent was Ford. Secret takeover talks began early in 1986, came into the open in May 1986, and by June the IRI was reportedly willing to sell out. At which time – and in typically Italian manner – the politicians got involved, suggesting that it was scandalous that control of the company should move outside Italy. Without appearing to do so, they then began to make it awkward for Ford (which thought it already had a deal), and began to encourage Fiat to take over instead.

Even so, by August 1986 a Ford–Alfa deal was said to be close; in September the deal was reputedly already done; yet in October an unseemly and bad-mouthed bidding battle took place between Ford and Fiat.

Once Fiat got involved, and with the matter of 'Italian honour' at stake, the odds tipped smartly towards a home victory. Sure enough, in November 1986 Fiat announced that it had agreed to buy Alfa Romeo for the mind-bending sum of £3.9 billion. Fiat's bosses insisted that they had been pushed into this deal by the Italian authorities – but they would say that, wouldn't they?

Fiat's move to rationalize Alfa Romeo was swift and far reaching. By the early 1990s, the famous four-cylinder twin-cam engine (as used in Giuliettas from the 1950s) had been laid to rest, as had the last of the Sud/33/Sprint range. The coupé/Spider cars which followed not only had entirely different engines and transmissions, but were front-wheel-drive, too.

8 Fiat and Rationalization – The Aftermath

There is no point speculating about the sporting cars Alfa Romeo might have wanted to make in the 1990s, for after Fiat took control at the end of 1986, it soon set out to impose its own will on the Milan-based firm, as it had done with Lancia in the 1970s and 1980s.

Even so, it is worth recalling the status of Alfa Romeo's sporting cars in 1986. Although there were three different models still in production, in technical and styling terms all were getting old:

- The Alfasud Sprint had been on the market for ten years, its engine already enlarged to the limit, at 1,717cc.
- The 2000 Spider, much-modified over the years, had been on sale since 1966. Little more, except yet another facelift perhaps, could be done with it.
- The Alfetta GT Coupé, now with top-of-the-range V6 engine, had already been on sale for twelve years. Like other sporting Alfas, it did not change much in the 1980s – the V6 engine was adopted in 1980, and there were no style changes of any type.

In the 1980s, in fact, Alfa Romeo almost ignored its sporting cars, preferring to concentrate its new-model efforts on saloons, estate cars and hatchbacks. In chronological order, the 33 appeared in 1983, the 90 in 1984 and the 75 in 1985. Not only that, but the company's major technical 'building blocks' – its engines and transmissions – were ageing. In some ways it was the classic case of a long-established company, which was gradually sliding into trouble, trading on a fine heritage but unable to generate the profit and the cashflow to invest in its future.

The factory in southern Italy (where Alfasud assembly had been concentrated in the 1970s and 1980s) had never operated at full stretch, which meant that Alfa production was, at best, static – 176,000 in 1982, 200,000 in 1983 and 1984, 158,000 in 1985 and 168,000 in 1986. Worse, because the joint project with Nissan – the Nissan-bodied/Alfa-engined Arna model – had been such a conspicuous failure, there was little optimism about the future.

On the other hand, Alfa's new owner, Fiat, Italy's manufacturing colossus, was buoyant, building ten times as many cars – along with overseeing Lancia, Autobianchi and Ferrari – plus thousands of trucks, and tractors, and aircraft, and it was not short of demand, profitable businesses or cash. But Fiat could not turn round Alfa Romeo's fortunes at once. To coin a famous phrase from the joke books: 'The impossible we do at once. Miracles take a little time'. And not even the financial and industrial muscle of Fiat could beat that quip.

By the end of 1988, the smart front-wheel-drive 164 saloon had appeared, though there was no immediate sign of any sporting derivative to come from that substantial base. That was the good news. The sad news was that the last of the Alfetta GTs had been produced (Alfa needed all the space it could get at Arese for the 164 to be built). The amazing news was that, purely for fun, it seemed, Fiat had allowed Alfa Romeo the indulgence of launching the Zagato-manufactured SZ Coupé.

And more was to come. The following is an account of the way in which Fiat replaced the cars that have been described so affectionately in this book.

SZ Coupé and RZ Convertible

The SZ Coupé was a car that immediately created strong impressions. No sooner had enthusiasts clapped eyes on it than they either hated it or loved it. The chassis itself, complete with a 210bhp/2,959cc V6 engine (which was an enlarged version of that used in the 1980s in the Alfetta GTV6), was fine, responsive and ultra-sporting. It was the styling of the two-seater which caused such controversy.

The coachbuilding specialist, Zagato, however, who was scheduled to manufacture the cars, didn't mind that. Better for a new model to be talked about, it concluded, than for it to be ignored completely. And, in any case, it wasn't Zagato's risk. Smiling sweetly, it accepted hundreds of advance deposits (which underwrote its tooling costs for creating the exotic-material panels) and prepared to deliver cars.

Some called the new car ugly, some said they couldn't understand how or why, but in the end they were proved wrong. The fastback style was certainly startling, and it grabbed everyone's attention in a way that Giugiaro's latest offerings could never have done.

Was it because the flanks were too flat, maybe? Or because there were six headlamps instead of

With the SZ coupé of 1989, Alfa set out to startle rather than seduce.

four, and these were rectangular instead of circular? Or because the boot was tiny and full of spare wheel? But it wasn't meant to be practical; it was meant to be an indulgence, pure and simple. Despite all this, the efficiency of the shape must, at least, have been reasonably 'clean', for an SZ could reach at least 150mph (240kph), making a good deal of sound and fury along the way.

Previewed in 1989, the SZ prompted a great deal of speculation. Why had Zagato, it was asked, produced such an aggressive style? Why was this a car which was only to be built with one type of engine – the most expensive that Alfa currently manufactured? Why was there not to be

an open-top version?

What was not clear at this early stage was that it was Alfa's Centro Stile department (the factory's own, in other words) which had shaped the car. Zagato only got the job of making the car because they needed the work! It was not a job that the Alfa factory would ever have wanted to tackle in any case, for once the platform and running gear had been supplied – the rolling chassis, in effect – the hard work began. It wasn't just that this was to be a distinctly limited-production machine, but that the body shell was built from a mixture of pressed-steel, hand-formed steel, plastic, and high-tech carbon-fibre mouldings. This,

The SZ (sometimes called ES30) looked angular rather than sinuous. The latest type of 3-litre V6 was under the skin.

In spite of the hatchback looks, the SZ was a pure coupé with a fixed rear window. A two-seater only, it also had a great deal of stowage space.

Visually, this is the SZ's most appealing angle; there are no signs of the 75 saloon ancestry on which it was based.

of course, would make it a car one could boast about, but it very cleverly hid the more mainstream components from view.

The fact was that the chassis/platform itself, and the running gear attached to it, were well established. Based on that of the existing Alfa Romeo 75 saloon (a pre-Fiat model which had itself only been announced in 1985), this meant that in its heritage it was also a derivation of the Alfetta of 1972 (*see* page 122). The SZ, in other words, was not much more than a dressed-up, modernized Alfetta GTV6, for it shared the same front engine/rear transaxle layout, the same basic front suspension (now with coil-over-shocks rather than torsion bars), and the same De Dion axle/coil-spring rear end.

Its wheelbase was exactly the same as that of the 75 saloon, but 4.3in (110mm) longer than that of the old Alfetta GTV6. The 2,959cc V6 engine produced 210bhp, whereas the last of the Alfetta GTV6s had a very close relative, a 2,492cc/160bhp V6. The basic difference between the two engines was that with the same cylinder block, the bore/stroke dimensions had been enlarged – from 88 × 68.3mm to 93 × 72.6mm.

Which goes some way to explaining why the Alfetta GT, with its unique Alfa-manufactured/Giugiaro-styled coupé body shell was no longer in production. Not only had it reached the end of its useful development life by 1987, but it could not have been updated to take the SZ's engine, and matched in all dynamic effects.

Even so, Alfa Romeo never looked on the new SZ as a long-life project and, right from the start, it was decided to limit production to just 1,000 examples and not make it available to the North American market. Anyone wanting to buy a car in Europe had to put down a substantial deposit in advance – this was said to be at least £3,000 (approximately $5,000) – and wait.

Deliveries did not begin until the last months of 1989, and this was very fortunate for both Alfa Romeo and Zagato. This was the moment when the 'collectors' car' boom was at its absolute peak, when almost any type of fast/limited-production/high-performance machine would find a market. Two or three years later, after the 'investment' bubble had burst, demand fell away considerably.

No matter. In 1990 and 1991 it sold steadily

until the 1,000 target had been reached. Then, in 1992, Alfa trumped their own ace by introducing the RZ derivative, which was a two-seater convertible version of the same package, with the same front-end style, the same uncompromising flat flanks, but now with a soft-top. The windscreen had been cropped a little, the soft-top had to be erected manually, but the effect, and the character, were still familiar.

It was enough. Zagato originally planned to make only 350, reputedly upped that to 800, and closed down the entire project a year or so later. Everyone, it seemed – Alfa enthusiasts, Fiat, and especially the accountants who had to decide whether it had been profitable – was happy.

GTV and Spider

If ever there were cars which could replace the 1960s-type Giulia Sprint GTV and Spider models in spirit, here they were. Styled on a carefully

commonized design base (below the waistline and ahead of the windscreen, the two cars – open and closed – used the same panels and sub-assemblies), these were squat, purposeful, beautifully detailed, and above all sporting Alfa Romeos with exactly the sort of appeal that had suited the Giulia family so well in the past.

There was, however, a major difference. Here, for the first time, were medium-sized sporty Alfas that had transverse engines and front-wheel-drive. They were not the first transverse-engined Alfas – the 164 of 1987 had taken that honour – but they were the first with sporting ambitions. Here, too, was a sporty Alfa developed around the chassis and platform of another make of car – that of the Fiat Tipo/Lancia Dedra family.

But there was more to it than that, which emphasizes just how much interlinked support and activity existed in Italy's motor industry at the time. In this case, neither Bertone (Giulia) nor Giugiaro (Alfetta GT/Sprint GT) were involved.

'GTV' might be a familiar title, but in 1994 the new Fiat-inspired generation was very different from the old. Not only was the style to be shared with an open-top Spider, but there was front-wheel drive, too.

Conceived by a Lancia design chief, who worked with the guidance of Pininfarina, the GTV was smart and definitely unique in its looks, yet the platform was based on that of a Fiat layout.

The twin-overhead camshaft twin-spark engine, which had found a home in so many Alfa Romeos since the mid-1990s, was a new Fiat corporate layout, having no links with the famous old Giulietta/Giulia engine.

From this angle, the common styling heritage of the new Spider and GTV of 1994 is obvious. The entire platform, mechanical layout, front-end, doors and general proportions were the same.

In 1994 the new GTV/Spider twins shared this stubby, high-tail layout; totally different from any Alfa shape that had gone before.

Amazingly, the GTV/Spider's front-end included four tiny headlamps which produced a remarkable beam pattern. Although there was still a hint of Alfa's traditional 'shield' front grille, it had been incorporated into the huge front pressing. This, in fact, is the 24V 3.0-litre V6-engined type.

At Fiat's direction, the original style of the twins – coupé and Spider – had been evolved in the Pininfarina studio by Fiat's Lancia Studio Chief Enrico Fumia in 1990. It was only when Fiat officially signed off the new twins for production that Alfa Romeo finally took them in hand for what might be called 'productionization', and to complete the development of every little detail.

For the first time ever, Alfa Romeo had elected to make new tin-top and open-top cars on the same length of wheelbase, on the same platform, on the same front-end, A-pillars, doors and lower rear panels. As a reminder, not only did the sporty Giulietta and Giulia coupés look entirely different from their contemporary Spiders, they were even styled in different design houses (Bertone and Pininfarina, respectively).

Technically, there were no links with old-type Alfa coupés. By using a Fiat Tipo-based platform and front-wheel drive, there could not be. The monocoque platform itself, complete with a transversely-positioned engine, was totally different from anything seen under previous classic Alfa Romeo coupés – and so was the running gear.

Independent rear suspension – multi-links and coil springs – was one innovation, but it was the four-cylinder engine and the five-speed transmission that matched it which broke so many ties with the old Spider. Instead of the famous old 8-valve twin-cam, here was a new, 16-valve, twin-spark, twin-cam 1,969cc power unit, complete with Lanchester-style counter-rotating balancer shafts in a cast-iron cylinder block. Not only was this more powerful than the old engine could ever have been – even in its initial fuel-injected

Late 1990s/early 2000s GTVs and Spiders shared this well-equipped facia/instrument panel/seating layout. There is no getting away from airbags in the steering wheel and ahead of the passenger these days.

This may be the final flowering of the famous V6 engine, as fitted to GTV and Spider models as the twenty-first century opened: 3 litres, twin-cam heads, 24 valves, a trouble-free 220bhp, and a magnificent sound.

form, it produced 150bhp at 6,200rpm – but it was just one of a multitude of derivatives of Fiat's modern corporate power unit. In 1995, when seen in the GTV/Spider, it was still a novelty, but by 2000 one or other type – four-cylinder or five-cylinder, in a number of different sizes – was being used in no fewer than fourteen different Alfas, Fiats and Lancias.

Right from the start, too, there was the higher-priced option of a 2,959cc V6 engine, and by the end of the decade this had been joined by smaller four-cylinder types, and by modern, twin-cam-headed derivatives of the V6, plus a six-speed gearbox. This was, in other words, a typical multi-faceted Alfa Romeo programme which squeezed every possible combination from one body structure and the corporate stock of engines. Nothing new there, you might say … And the best news of all was that Fiat showed no signs of wanting to destroy Alfa's sporting heritage.

Index